A blueprint is a guide

Ida Engholm

Quick guide to design thinking

Strandberg Publishing

Published with generous support from

Danish Arts
Foundation

 The Royal Danish Academy of Fine Arts,
Schools of Architecture, Design and Conservation

Queen Margrethe and Prince Henrik's Foundation

Thanks to Mathilde Aggebo and Martin Sønderlev Christensen,
the Royal Danish Academy of Fine Arts, School of Design, for
supporting this book. Thanks also to my research assistant, now
Ph.D student, Anna Bascuñan Skaarup, for her tremendous help
with completing this book.

Series editors

Ida Engholm and Mads Nygaard Folkmann

Chapter 1
Design as thinking and practice

This book discusses the nature of design thinking from various perspectives, from within and outside design practice. It is intended as a quick guide offering an overview of the many different under-standings and approaches that characterise design thinking as a research and practice field.

The point of departure for the book is the current and increasing popularity of design thinking across a growing number of industries and sectors. Design thinking has become the new buzzword in the business and management literature. It is described on the cover of *Harvard Business Review* as 'an approach to devise strategy and management change' and highlighted as a popular innovation method by a growing number of business analysist, as well as concultancy firms, that are including design thinking in their service portfolio.[1]

Design thinking and design doing are interrelated activities in design practice.

Due to this growing interest in design thinking, the value of design is increasingly widely recognised. However, the versions of design thinking that are currently being circulated in much of the management literature and by many consultancy firms are fairly simplistic, compared to the understanding that characterises both contemporary and historical professional design research and practice. Thus, the debate about the potential applicability and benefits of design thinking calls for greater nuance.

> An underlying assumption of this book is that it is not meaningful to speak of design thinking without also considering design practice. 'Design thinking' and 'design doing' are interrelated in the practical application of design thinking.[2] It is the highly productive exchanges between the design practitioners' thinking and doing and their simultaneously conceptualising and materialising capacity that give design thinking its unique character.

In a time when companies increasingly focus on creativity and innovation, design thinking can offer specific approaches that facilitate these transformative processes. In relation to the major challenges the world is currently facing, design thinking also offers a tool for reflecting on and redeveloping society in more socially and environmentally sustainable directions on different scales. Design thinking can help us transform our surroundings and, by extension, ourselves.

To paraphrase the pioneering design thinker Victor Papanek, design thinking manifested as materialised design is one of the most powerful tools at humanity's disposal. That requires us to use this tool thoughtfully and with compassion.[3]

1.1.
Design thinking –
approaches and positions

The field of design thinking comprises a diverse range of understandings with roots in widely different theoretical approaches and methodological practices. In a literature study on design thinking, the design researcher Lucy Kimbell presents a helpful model that identifies several different incarnations of the concept. Kimbell's model defines three specific approaches to design thinking, visually represented in three columns.

In the view represented in the first column, 'Design thinking as a cognitive style', design thinking is defined as an expertise that is largely the reserve of trained designers. The focus is on designers' particular competences and ways of working and thinking, and design thinking is regarded as a certain 'cognitive style'. This style manifests itself as 'reflection-in-action', to quote a term coined by the design theorist Donald Schön: a mode of thinking that engages in an active and reflective dialogue with the given material or situation.

Another key concept is 'abductive thinking', which is defined as conjecturing and propositional approaches to idea generation and design development. This form of thinking differs from the deductive and inductive approaches that we find in traditional scientific methods aimed at generating knowledge. The benefit of this cognitive style is that through practice, designers acquire a particular kind of knowledge that is both reflective and embodied, a 'designerly way of knowing', as coined by the design theorist Nigel Cross.

In this view, the subject matter of design expertise relates mainly to traditional design disciplines, such as industrial design and graphic communication but also to various forms of material or technological mastery within design-related fields. In recent years, we have seen a growing focus on new interdisciplinary design fields, such as strategic design and service design, with the aim of exploring the role of trained designers' form-oriented approaches to design thinking. In this view, the focus is typically on 'designerly thinking', for example in the development of services, and were the premise is that the role of trained designers is to facilitate the processes with a focus on conceptualising and materialising specific solutions.[4]

Positions in design thinking. Adapted version of the design researcher Lucy Kimbell's model, which identifies the three above-mentioned approaches to design thinking.[5]

	DESIGN THINKING AS A COGNITIVE STYLE	DESIGN THINKING AS A GENERAL THEORY OF DESIGN	DESIGN THINKING AS AN ORGANISATIONAL RESOURCE
FOCUS	INDIVIDUAL DESIGNERS, ESPECIALLY EXPERTS	DESIGN AS A FIELD OR DISCIPLINE	BUSINESSES AND OTHER ORGANISATIONS IN NEED OF INNOVATION
DESIGN'S PURPOSE	PROBLEM-SOLVING	TAMING WICKED PROBLEMS	INNOVATION
KEY CONCEPTS	DESIGN ABILITY AS A FORM OF INTELLIGENCE; REFLECTION-IN-ACTION, ABDUCTIVE THINKING	DESIGN HAS NO SPECIAL SUBJECT MATTER OF ITS OWN	VISUALISATION, PROTOTYPING, EMPATHY, INTEGRATIVE THINKING, ABDUCTIVE THINKING
NATURE OF DESIGN PROBLEMS	DESIGN PROBLEMS ARE ILL-STRUCTURED, PROBLEM AND SOLUTION CO-EVOLVE	DESIGN PROBLEMS ARE WICKED PROBLEMS	ORGANISATIONAL PROBLEMS ARE DESIGN PROBLEMS
SITES OF DESIGN EXPERTISE AND ACTIVITY	TRADITIONAL DESIGN DISCIPLINES	FOUR ORDERS OF DESIGN	ANY CONTEXT FROM HEALTHCARE TO ACCESS TO CLEAN WATER.
KEY TEXTS	CROSS 1982; SCHÖN 1983; ROWE [1987] 1998; LAWSON 1997; CROSS 2006; DORST 2006	BUCHANAN 1992	DUNNE AND MARTIN 2006; BAUER AND EAGAN 2008; BROWN 2009; MARTIN 2009; BROWN & WYATT 2010.

The three columns in Kimbell's model represent different approaches to design thinking that are not inherently in competition and which may, in principle, continue to develop in parallel. However, there is no doubt that there is a considerable potential for dialogue between the approaches aimed at accumulating further theoretical and methodological knowledge within both design and management contexts, thus contributing to increased cross-disciplinary cooperation.

The second column, 'Design thinking as a general theory of design', represents reflections that have been part of design research since design became a scientific discipline during the 1960s, when the main focus was on debating the underlying methodology and theory of science that define design as a discipline. This position has also been called the 'design studies tradition' with reference, in part, to anthologies published during the mid 1990s, edited by design researchers Richard Buchanan and Victor Margolin, with the purpose of initiating a debate about the scientific and theoretical foundations of the design discipline and subsequently followed up by articles, conferences and magazines, including, for example, the journal *Design Issues*.

In this variant of design thinking studies too, the trained designer is seen as occupying a special position, but the areas of design expertise are more broadly defined than in the approaches represented in the first column. Here, the emphasis is on developing a general theory of design with the understanding that various disciplines may be involved both in designing and in generating knowledge about design. The primary focus is on theoretical discussions of design thinking as a combined research and practice field, where design and design thinking may also be manifested as a distributed activity that involves multiple areas of expertise. Hence, studies of design and design thinking must also, naturally, have a multidisciplinary basis.

Although the two columns represent different views of the scope of design, they still represent a fairly coherent body of knowledge with several overlaps and cross references.[6] Both areas aim to develop design research that is not limited to the humanities, the social sciences, the technical and natural sciences or, for that matter, to an interdisciplinary mix of these different fields. Rather, they aim for a particular research and knowledge form that is unique to design as a discipline and related to design thinking as a research and practice field.[7] This refers to the particular 'design knowledge', which in the design studies tradition is a form of knowledge that can be generated by many different disciplines or professions to the benefit of design as a discipline.

The third and last column in the model represents the more recent management/business-oriented versions of design thinking. In this view, design thinking is mainly regarded as an organisational resource and as more or less synonymous with innovation. The idea here is that design thinking is a particular perceptual and practical approach that is derived from the design discipline but which can, in principle, be learned by anyone and is not only the reserve of trained designers. Design expertise thus applies to any context or activity aimed at planning or conceptualisation — from organisational development to healthcare to ensuring access to clean water.

In Kimbell's model, the management/business-oriented
approaches are primarily associated with the environment around
Stanford University and the design firm IDEO. As documented by
Kimbell's work and other meta-studies of the literature on design
thinking, most of the publications within this framework are of a
popular and how-to-oriented nature and have a limited research
base.[8] Another remarkable feature is that many of the publications
written by authors with a research background make only limited
reference to the rich theoretical and methodological research
that has been conducted from the 1960s within the design
profession.[9] However, since 2008, the Hasso Plattner Design
Thinking Research Foundation has funded a research environment
associated with the d.school programmes at Stanford University
and Potsdam University, and since 2011, the universities have
published several yearbooks in the form of anthologies that document the research in the two academic environments. The focus
here is on technical, mercantile and human aspects of innovation
with design thinking at the core, but several studies also address
and discuss aspects of design research that relate to the design
profession and have thus contributed to an early dialogue between
the different positions.

1.2.
Ways of speaking and thinking about design thinking

In order to take a more in-depth look at the various positions within design thinking, in the following I will present some of the research studies and publications that have defined the field so far. To that end, I will now turn to the design researchers Ulla Johansson-Sköldberg, Jill Woodilla and Mehves Cetinkaya's (hereafter Johansson-Sköldberg et al.) distinction between two main discourses in the design thinking literature: the 'design and designerly thinking discourse' and the 'management discourse on design thinking'. In other contexts, the latter has also been called 'the traditional design thinking approach' and 'the new design thinking movement'.[10]

The term 'Design and designerly thinking' is used by Johansson-Sköldberg et al. as a general term for the approaches that Kimbell places in the left and middle columns in her model. They refer, respectively, to practice-based theories on how designers think and work and to theoretical scientific representations of design thinking as a field.[11] In line with Kimbell's third column, Johansson-Sköldberg et al.'s 'management discourses' refer to design thinking that is described and practised outside a professional design context. In this context, the term 'discourse' refers to a particular way of speaking about and understanding design thinking.

In **Chapter 2**, I take a closer look at 'design and designerly thinking discourses', the approach that accounts for most of the research literature on design thinking. This includes examining the sub-discourses in the field. The discourses are represented by agenda-setting theorists and 'founding fathers'.

In **Chapter 3**, I focus on the 'management discourse on design thinking', which is a much younger field that so far has only accumulated a limited research base. As it is thus too soon to attempt to describe a fully developed research landscape, this chapter is shorter than Chapter 2.

Chapter 4 opens with an outline of the various design thinking approaches with an emphasis on current topics of debate related to design thinking across positions and approaches. The chapter can also be read as a call for action to design researchers and design thinking practitioners, encouraging more cross-disciplinary dialogue and, not least, a stronger engagement in the major challenges facing the world.

DESIGN AND DESIGNERLY THINKING DISCOURSES	MANAGEMENT DISCOURSE ON DESIGN THINKING
CHAPTER 2	CHAPTER 3

1.3.
Design is about creating what does not exist yet

Like 'design thinking', 'design' is an expansive concept with many different meanings and understandings. The word has its origins in the Latin *designare*, which means, in part, to designate or mark out. In a contemporary understanding, the term generally means to explore and propose what does not exist yet: conceiving of and realising new things.[12] The design theorist Mads Nygaard Folkmann has described the concept of design as covering a span between a general and a specific, disciplinary perspective.[13]

From a general perspective, the practice of design, in principle, dates back to human beings' earliest interventions into their natural environment. Thus, all types of tools may be seen as manifestations of design.[14] From a disciplinary perspective, creating the new is associated with the design profession, which emerged with the advance of industrialisation and mass production in the mid 18th century. In this development, making went from a purely craft-based to a conceptualising activity aimed at shaping ideas and templates for things with a view to subsequent production. Thus, design came to be about form and design intentions.[15] Below, the general and the disciplinary design understandings are represented by quotes from early design thinkers.

'Everyone designs who devises courses of action aimed at changing existing situations into preferred ones.'
Herbert A. Simon, 1969.

'Design is 'the process of inventing physical things which display new physical order, organization, form in response to function. The ultimate object of design is form.'
Christopher Alexander, 1971.

Simon's and Alexander's statements represent two key positions that continue to define one of the main axes in the debate about the concept of design. This axis is also present, across positions and approaches, in reflections on what design thinking is and who is entitled to practise it.

The Nobel economist Herbert A. Simon famously wrote in 1969 that design is about devising a course of action aimed at 'changing existing situations into preferred ones'. In this sense, design is not the reserve of designers but can, in principle, be practiced by anyone.[16] In contrast to this broad notion, the architect and design theorist Christopher Alexander (1964) claims that 'the ultimate object of design is form'. In this sense, design is thus primarily associated with a profession of trained designers and architects.[17]

SOLUTION

Design builds a bridge between what exists and the new that is yet to be developed. The design researcher Bryan Lawson describes the designer's mission as follows: 'The designer has a prescriptive rather than descriptive job. Unlike scientists who describe how the world is, designers suggest how it might be.'[18]

Chapter 2
Design and designerly thinking discourses

The approaches associated with 'design and designerly thinking' broadly capture academic reflections on the practice of professional designers (including practical talents and competences) on how to interpret and characterise designers' often nonverbal competences.

Designerly thinking connects theory and practice from a design perspective and is thus anchored in the research-based field of design.[19] In disciplinary terms, the discourse is defined by a diverse field of trained designers, architects, design historians, technologists, philosophers of science, sociologists of professions and so forth. With their varied theoretical and methodological backgrounds, they have contributed to the development of different understandings of designers' ways of working and thinking.

2.1.
Design and designerly thinking as a science of the artificial

Historically, the discourse related to design and designerly thinking can be traced back to early reflections on designers' methods during the 1960s. The interest in design methods emerged in parallel with the major technological and scientific breakthroughs that were made during and just after the Second World War. A key factor was the invention of the computer and, closely associated with this breakthrough, new systems and complexity theories that seemed to address every conceivable aspect of the world — from the understanding of the human body as a self-organising system of signals to visions of artificial machine intelligence and robots with the potential to relieve human beings of a wide range of working tasks.

When everything is design. Buckminster Fuller's air ocean town plan diagram (1927) with an early comment on globalisation and the consequences of a maladaptive design development: 'United we stand, divided we fall.' Below: Fuller's sketch for a 'hemispherical dome' over Manhattan from 1962 with a two-mile diameter. The geodesic dome would weigh 80,000 tons, be constructed of five-ton sections and be assembled by helicopters over a period of three months. The dome structure itself was to be inhabitable. It was to act as a solar collector in winter and a heat shield in summer. The cost would be USD 200 million, but Fuller believed it would pay for itself by reducing the costs of air-conditioning, waste collection, snow removal and loss of earnings due to colds and other respiratory infections.

These ambitious ideas were reflected, for example, in megalo-
maniacal design projects, such as the design theorist and inventor
Buckminster Fuller's visionary projects, including the 'dome over
Manhattan' and his idea of 'the architect as world planner'.[20] Later,
the design theorist Otl Aicher wrote *The World as Design.* Design,
in all its variants, took a giant leap forward towards new degrees
of complexity during the initial decades following the Second
World War.

> In 1969, Herbert A. Simon wrote *The Sciences of the Artificial*,
> which introduced design as a methodical, precise and technical
> activity aimed at 'changing existing situations into preferred ones'
> in all types of contexts, particularly technical and scientific ones,
> where a rational form of management could be exercised.[21] Simon
> is widely regarded as one of the 'founding fathers' of academic
> studies of design thinking and may also be seen as one of the key
> figures behind 'design and designerly thinking discourses'.[22]

Although Simon never explicitly used the term 'design thinking',
his cognitive approach to decision-making and his oft-quoted
definition of design as the transformation of existing conditions into
preferred ones form important references for the academic literature on design thinking.[23] In Simon's view, design was essentially
about examining and exploring 'the possible'; thus, design mainly
dealt with how the world 'could' or 'should be', unlike other sciences,
which dealt with the existing reality.[24] According to Simon, design
includes all the deliberate activities needed to create artefacts,
and his research was in itself an example of the new broad scope
of activities, his studies spanning from artificial intelligence to
management to design, psychology, sociology and economics,
problem-solving, decision-making and complexity theory.

> Thus, he not only articulated a normative goal of design —
> 'to improve existing situations' — but also a cross-disciplinary
> practice aimed at developing the artificial: the man-made world.
> That required an applied complexity, which may be seen as the
> overriding purpose of Simon's science of the artificial — a science
> that, broadly speaking, came to address how the man-made world
> could or should be developed by means of design. This implied a
> normative requirement that, in its insistence on being a 'science
> of the possible', introduced an alternative to the descriptive
> approaches of the natural sciences in favour of an interest in
> what could or should be different.

From a philosophical point of view, Simon's ambition of developing a science of the possible seemed to imply a tension between the present (what is) and the future (what could or should be). This tension created a melting pot of possibilities that, in Simon's understanding, was driven by rationalist expectations of systems theory and early computer research, which necessarily required an intentional appropriateness in the possible solutions.

Fuller, who was a contemporary of Simon's, similarly advocated an intentional approach to the man-made world, which was to be designed to serve human needs as efficiently as possible. From an early time, however, Fuller was aware of the dangers of a maladaptive design development, which would have harmful repercussions for nature and, thus, for humanity. To Fuller, the purpose of design had to be 'to make the world work for 100% of humanity in the shortest possible time through spontaneous cooperation without ecological offence or the disadvantage of anyone,' as he writes in an early example of a focus on sustainability in design thinking. In light of the global environmental challenges we face today, we must, sadly, acknowledge that this vision has not been universally embraced.

2.2.
Design and designerly thinking as methodology

The scientific interest in design creation from Simon, Alexander and others marked a shift towards more academic and theoretical thinking about design. Around the time of the release of Simon's *The Sciences of the Artificial* (1969) there were discussions in Europe and the United States about how to strengthen the design discipline through an increased emphasis on theoretical and methodological reflection. This development led to a beginning shift in focus from design products to design methods.

As early as the late 1950s, the famous Hochschule für Gestaltung Ulm (Ulm School of Design) in Germany introduced an academic curriculum of design with an enhanced focus on design methodology. The school, which was founded in 1953 as a modern successor to the Bauhaus School, operated with the notion that designers would engage in creating products but would also be able to bring their skills to bear in the increasingly complex contexts of the industrial society. Through increased reflection on methods, designers would refine their ability to lead, manage and engage in complex design processes that brought together several different areas of expertise.

In 1962, the first academic conference on design methods was held in England, with Alexander and the architect John Christopher Jones among the organisers. The stated purpose of the conference was to establish institutionalised practices for knowledge sharing within design and academically founded thinking about design methods.[25] In recent design research studies, the conference is recognised as the cornerstone of the so-called Design Method movement and a key influence on design and designerly thinking discourses. The event was in part inspired by the field of project management, which was under development as an academic discipline during the 1960s with a focus on developing methods for more efficient and goal-driven projects in the highly industrialised society.

Design as a coordinating activity. The famous Hochschule für Gestaltung in Ulm pioneered the use of academic reflection on designers' ways of working. This was driven by a call for a more systematic approach and a greater awareness of methods in relation to the designer's role in the highly industrialised post-war society. In this effort, the more artistic approach that had originally defined the designers' self-image was to be replaced by a more team-oriented design approach. Tomas Maldonado, the rector of the Ulm School, wrote about the major challenges facing designers: 'The designer has to be a coordinator. His responsibility will be that of coordinating the diverse requirements from the company's production department and the coming users in close cooperation with a large number of specialists. The designer has the ultimate responsibility for both optimal productivity in manufacturing and the user's maximal satisfaction in a cultural sense and with regard to the materials.'[26]

Jones, whose model is shown below, defined design as a domain of rational problem-solving, manifested through a method that broke the design process down to three distinct phases: analysis, synthesis and evaluation. In later studies, this is often referred to as the generic model of the design process, which current process presentations are seen as elaborations on.[27] According to Jones, practising designers were to move from one phase to the next in a linear progression. First, exhaustive lists of demands and challenges related to the problem at hand, then a synthesis — which solution to pick? — and finally evaluation and execution.

Later meta-studies of the early academic literature on design methods have described these early approaches as 'first-generation methods'.[28] A characteristic of these early studies is a goal of applying linear methods with a focus on goal-driven management and a general idea of being able to develop universal models to guide designers in a wide variety of tasks.

1. ANALYSIS

1.1 GENERAL LIST OF FACTORS THAT AFFECT THE PRODUCT AND ITS REQUIREMENTS
1.2 CLASSIFICATION OF FACTORS
1.3 SOURCES OF INFORMATION REGARDING THE DESIGN
1.4 INTERACTION BETWEEN FACTORS
1.5 SPECIFICATION OF REQUIRE-MENTS FOR THE DESIGN
1.6 REACHING AGREEMENTS BETWEEN THE INVOLVED PARTNERS

2. SYNTHESIS

2.1 CREATIVE THOUGHT PROCESSES
2.2 PARTIAL SOLUTIONS
2.3 COMBINATION OF PARTIAL SOLUTIONS
2.4 OVERVIEW OF POTENTIAL SOLUTIONS – DECISION-MAKING

3. EVALUATION

3.1 METHOD OF EVALUATING THE PRODUCT
3.2 EVALUATING PRODUCTION OUTPUT AND SALES

A method of systematic design. During the 1970s, John Christopher Jones launched one of the best-known and most influential versions of a 'first-generation method-ology'. Three stages were required to achieve a fully rationalised design method: 1) Analysis: brainstorming and formulating information, demands and factors and a reduction of these to definable characteristics; 2) Synthesis: determining possible solution models based on connecting ideas from the analysis stage; 3) Evaluation: assessing how well the alternative solutions meet the demands for production and sales. Choice of solution.

2.3.
Design and designerly thinking as a way of problem-solving

During the early 1970s, several theorists began to realise that in the modern industrial society, design problems had become so complex that they could not be solved through rational, linear processes. In 1972, the design theorist Horst Rittel introduced the notion of 'wicked problems' as a key characteristic of modern design. He argued that most of the problems that scientists and engineers grapple with are 'tame' or 'benign'. The latter problems might involve solving a mathematical equation, analysing the structure of an unknown chemical compound or searching for a way to achieve checkmate in five moves — challenges where there is no ambiguity as to whether the task has been achieved, the problem solved.

By contrast, so-called wicked problems have no straightforward solution. Instead, their complexity increases, the more closely we examine them. The more we go into solution mode, the clearer it becomes that the complex or wicked problem cannot be solved with just one solution model. There is always a plurality of partial problems and solutions. One example Rittel offers is urban planning, such as the placement of a new motorway or how to bring down the crime rate in a troubled neighbourhood, tasks that he considers design problems. These problems call for non-linear approaches because they typically involve a complex mix of economic, technological and social changes that transform an area, dismantle well-established ground rules and render the future unpredictable. As illustrated by the drawing on the opposite page, input in the form of a design brief, a series of design speci- fications, can result in a wide variety of proposed solutions, which are difficult to predict. The complex problems Rittel outlines do not have one obvious solution but many possible ones.

Wicked problems. Design problems are often complex, and the process of solving them cannot be captured by a straightforward rational formula. According to Horst Rittel, solutions to wicked problems cannot be true or false, only good or bad. Through an iterative process where the problem definition and the possible solutions are determined in a mutual exchange, we can cut through the myriad demands and arrive at qualified proposals.

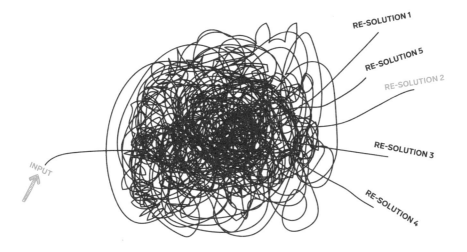

INPUT

RE-SOLUTION 1
RE-SOLUTION 5
RE-SOLUTION 2
RE-SOLUTION 3
RE-SOLUTION 4

The notion of wicked problems in design led to the development of what Rittel called 'second-generation methods', which treat problem-solving as the core driver of design and replace the linear understanding that is associated with first-generation methods with an iterative, looping approach to design development.[29] Rather than viewing the identification of the problem as an activity that primarily takes place during the first stage — analysis — as prescribed by first-generation methods, Rittel regarded the problem definition as a continuous process that unfolds in interrelated cycles of idea generation and solution development.

In 1992, Rittel's notion of wicked design problems was further developed by the design theorist Richard Buchanan. In the paper 'Wicked Problems in Design Thinking' he introduces a view of the design process as consisting of two distinct stages: an analytical stage focused on problem definition and a synthetising stage followed by summarising sequences of problem-solving.

The design process is iterative. In accordance with the conceptual core of second-generation methods, the design theorist Bernhard Bürdek's model of the design process shows how different stages of problem identification, analysis, idea development and evaluation are interrelated rather than unfolding along a linear path.[30]

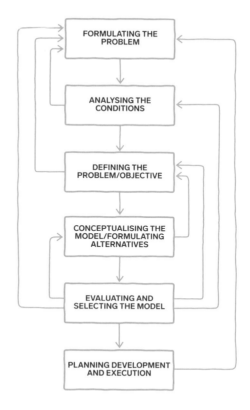

Buchanan also introduces the concept of 'placement' to describe the elements of contextualisation that are part of the design process. Placement, according to Buchanan, may be seen as a tool for 'shaping the design situation' in both intuitive and deliberate ways by eliciting insights from users who engage in the design situation and context.[31] In this approach, the formulation of the problem and of the solution go hand in hand, rather than unfolding in sequential stages.

Buchanan's process perspective reflects an ambition of achieving a deeper understanding of design thinking and requires a multi-perspective study. He proposes a common discussion of design as a field to integrate the various outcomes of studies in practice into an overall framework that is capable of managing the diverse nature of design. To Buchanan, design is not a distinct and specific subject field but a discipline that has a role to play in many different innovation and development contexts. The discipline and the innovation contexts where design thinking and design doing can contribute is determined by the design practitioner: 'Design problems are "indeterminate" and "wicked" because design has no special subject matter of its own apart from what a designer conceives it to be,' as Buchanan put it.[32]

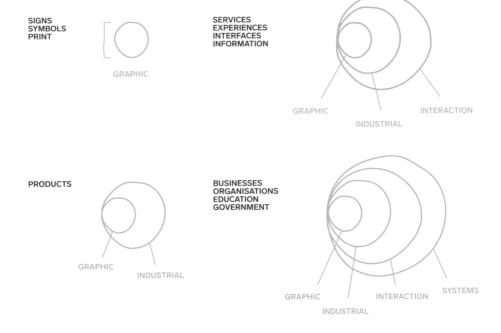

Four orders of design. According to Richard Buchanan (1992), design covers such a wide diversity of genres and qualities, products and manifesta-tions, systems and perspec-tives that the prospects of identifying a common discipline are limited. He proposes four orders of design and design thinking: 1) Symbolic and visual communication (graphic design); 2) material objects (industrial design); 3) activities and organisational services (service design); 4) complex systems or environments for living, working, playing or learning (interaction design).

In extension of this point, he suggests that design develops through 'four orders of design', where each 'order' is a place for rethinking and reconceiving the nature of design, not categories of a fixed meaning. Each 'order', as Buchanan sees it, is a platform for design activity and contains potentials for design thinking. Although Buchanan's model is aimed at a professional context, he sees design thinking as a wider area of expertise with a potential in most settings and argues that the combination of different orders can contribute to innovative design thinking. [33]

Problem and solutions are interrelated. An important insight in design thinking studies is that designers typically conceptualise and understand a problem concurrently with formulating solution proposals. This sets design thinking apart from, for example, traditional project management approaches, which typically begin with efforts to understand the problem and then proceed to attempts to solve it. In design thinking, the idea is that it is only through attempts to concretise a solution that one truly understands the nature of the problem. For example, it is only by modelling the digital prototype of an app that developers can see what it needs to be able to do, and how it should function. Similarly, it is only by sketching and creating tangible prototypes of a 'user journey' through an airport terminal that one can understand what the user experience should be like.

Rittel's and Buchanan's theories on design as a tool for solving complex problems are a key theme in the 'design and designerly thinking discourse' and have been further developed in several subsequent studies focusing on the problem-solving aspects of design. Here, the point that problem and solution are interrelated in design seems to constitute a key research focus. For example, Nigel Cross documents in recent studies that designers tend to understand a problem while they are formulating proposals for its solution. Thus, they often work with problem-solution pairs, rather than following a linear path from problem to solution.

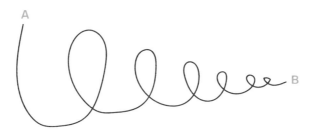

The notion that designers think in terms of problem-solution pairs rather than a linear chain of arguments leading from problem to solution implies that designers do not dwell very long on the task of defining problems. Cross has even called designers 'ill-behaved problem solvers'. His studies, on the other hand, document that it is this very ability to be anti-authoritarian and to know when the problem formulation is sufficient that makes designers so adept at spotting patterns and translating complex briefs into meaningful solutions. [34] Donald Norman summarises a similar point in his 2013 essay 'Rethinking Design Thinking', where he states that 'designers often attempt to solve problems about which they know nothing. I have also come to believe that in such ignorance lies great power: The ability to ask stupid questions'.[35]

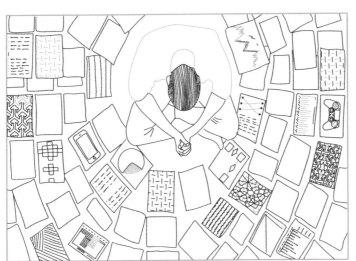

'Ill-behaved problem solvers'. Based on observation studies of designers, Nigel Cross concludes that designers tend to be slightly 'ill-behaved' in their approach to problem-solving. Competent designers, according to Cross, also typically seek to challenge both the problem and the most obvious solution rather than going with the first proposal that seems to fit the bill.

2.4.
Design and designerly thinking as practice epistemology

Another important sub-discourse in design thinking studies related to the design field deals with how trained designers think when they think. The interest in the cognitive dimensions of the design process grew particularly pronounced during the 1980s, when critical discussions of the limitations of the idealised process approaches in first- and second-generation methods led to a shift in focus from design methods to real-life processes.

This development also fuelled an interest in the way designers think and work in practice. While early design studies aimed to develop universal methods or general guidelines for design work, the focus now shifted to what was happening in the designer's mind: designers' thinking and perception. That laid the foundation for studies of so-called design cognition or design epistemology, which design method research calls third-generation methods, largely synonymous with Kimbell's first column, 'Design thinking as cognitive style' (see p. 13).

An important source of inspiration for this school of research was the work of the philosopher and sociologist Donald Schön. Based on philosophical reflections on the possibilities and limitations human perception with regard to design as a material or conceptual phenomenon, his influential book *The Reflective Practitioner* (1983) represented an empirical study of design thinking in practice. One of Schön's key points is that design thinking always occurs in a dialogue with a specific material or situation. The process of delimiting a problem or a task and developing a proposal for its solution unfolds in a mutual exchange — what Schön calls 'reflection-in-action'.

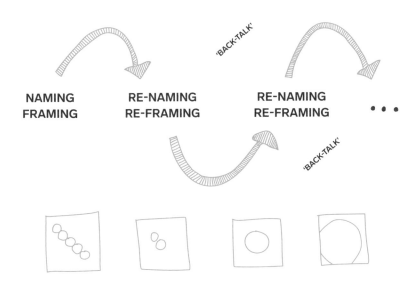

'BACK-TALK'

NAMING   **RE-NAMING**   **RE-NAMING**
FRAMING   **RE-FRAMING**   **RE-FRAMING**   • • •

'BACK-TALK'

Naming and framing. In Donald Schön's understanding, the design process is an almost herme- neutic activity, which begins with the identification of a challenge — so-called 'naming' and 'framing'. Next, the situation or practice responds, and a new reflec- tion occurs: 're-naming and re-framing'. The process repeats itself until a given goal has been achieved.

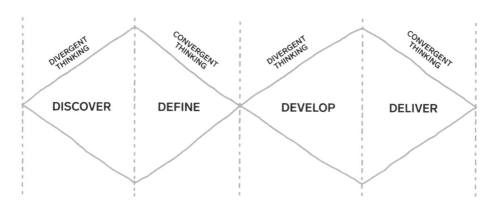

Design thinking as an exchange between opening and closing. A key focus in Donald Schön's work and, later, cognitive studies was the mindsets designers rely on in a process — a topic that was instrumental in shaping current design method studies. Here, the British Council's 'Double Diamond Model' illustrates the three typical (generic) stages of the design process: analysis, synthesis and execution, here in the alliteration of Discover, Define, Develop and Deliver. The point is that the designer alternates between an 'opening' (examining possibilities and ideas with a divergent, seeking and explorative mindset) and a 'closing' (convergent and synthesising mindset): two types of mindsets and behaviours that designers excel at, according to professional design studies.[36]

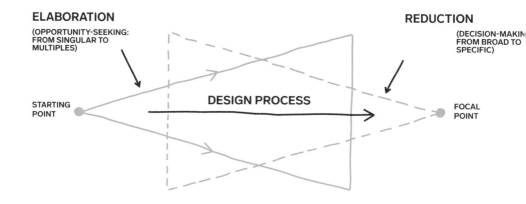

Glimpsing solutions in the design process. In a digital context, the user experience theorist and designer Bill Buxton has depicted the design process as an extracted picture that begins with elaboration and concludes with reduction; the process thus unfolds within this span. The breakthrough happens at the point where the axes intersect and the designer is able to glimpse the solution as the result of repeated cognitive opening and closing processes.[37]

2.5.
Design and designerly thinking as design cognition

Continuing the reflective tradition that was initiated by Donald Schön, the design researchers Cross and Lawson have, since the 1980s, conducted several empirical studies to examine how designers think and act.

Lawson's book *How Designers Think: The Design Process Demystified* has been reprinted several times since 1980, while Cross's research is published in many articles about 'designerly ways of knowing' and, most recently, in his book *Design Thinking* from 2011. Applying an ethnographic perspective, Cross's work aims to uncover what designers do during the design process, while Lawson's work is informed by cognitive psychology with the aim of understanding the creative design process and conducting and communicating design research in a form that is useful to designers in their work.

Cross and Lawson can both be regarded as part of the reflective tradition that was initiated by Schön. However, their writings belong in a different scientific tradition, as they take a practice-oriented approach, not least due to their architectural training. Thus, they convey their insights through examples, while Schön's work is informed mainly by a philosophical, epistemological perspective. Both Lawson and Cross use abductive thinking as a basis for arriving at understanding and generalisations based on observations and then identifying patterns that rest on and can be described through practical examples. They also both propose models for the design process. Lawson's model includes a number of process-driven steps that describe the complex process of designing,[38] while Cross offers procedural descriptions of the strategies creative designers appear to follow.[39]

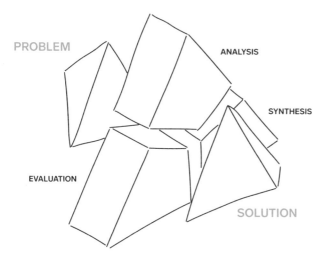

PROBLEM

ANALYSIS

SYNTHESIS

EVALUATION

SOLUTION

The components of a design process. In a shift away from the prescriptive models that characterised the early design method studies, Lawson offers an almost deconstructed view of the design process. His illustration has been described as a third-generation method due to its focus on dynamic real-life processes and on the importance of the cognitive dimensions of design work.[40] Lawson suggests that rather than adhering to an ideal method, designers should internalise and develop an awareness of the components that typically make up a design process. Thus, in a case of learning by doing, designers learn to identify the current mode or stage of a given process at any given moment. Knowing what action mode and mindset (for example, analysis, synthesis or evaluation) they are currently engaged in enables designers to navigate in the process and to lead others.

Design solution. Many empirical studies have documented that it is the capacity for creative, abductive formulation of proposals that makes designers so adept at quickly recognising patterns and reconciling complex requirements in a conceptualised design solution that makes sense in the intended context. However, it is only when design thinking results in an extraordinary material or immaterial form that the unique qualities of the way designers work are fully realised. One striking example of an extraordinary design solution is Utzon's design of the Sydney Opera House. The initial requirements were complex and diverse, as the building had to be a landmark for the city, contain multiple concert halls with outstanding acoustics and so forth. Utzon's unique design solution was inspired by a peeled orange. The solution reconciled multiple requirements and thus made sense on several levels. Today, the Opera House is an icon not just for Sydney but for Australia as a whole.[41]

In line with Cross's and Lawson's interest in design cognition, the Dutch design theorist Kees Dorst has examined the reasoning patterns behind design thinking. In the article 'The Nature of Design Thinking' (2010) he introduces the abductive approach as a critical aspect of how designers think. Compared to so-called deductive and inductive approaches — which he defines as being the core of analytic logic — abduction is characterised by a guesswork approach to examining a topic and suggesting what might be. Dorst further distinguishes between a general use of abduction (abduction-1) — which has to do with problem-solving and which, in his analysis, defines how engineers work — and a more advanced practice (abduction-2), which involves more unknown parameters and a parallel effort aimed at grasping both the problem and its solution.

Dorst sees the approach character-ising abduction-2 as the core of design thinking. According to Dorst, designers differ from other professions by combining analytical reasoning and general abduction with an approach aimed at creating proposals.[42]
He later renamed the two abductive ways of thinking 'normal abduction' and 'design abduction'.[43]

> In the debate about who has a 'patent' on practising design thinking, a key point of contention is whether the ability to frame and propose specific solutions is a particular design competence, or whether the capacity for both systematic and synthesising thinking is one that a wide range of professionals can acquire. According to Cross, professional designers need to be better at communicating how trained designers think about and work with design.[44]

When it comes to which groups of professionals are good at practising design thinking, proponents of a general understanding of design would argue that professionals from a wide range of backgrounds can learn to apply an abductive approach, framing problems and solutions in a back-and-forth process. In contrast, design thinkers with a professional design background, such as Lawson, Dorst and Cross, see this competence as being largely exclusive to designers. Because designers are trained and expe-rienced in letting the problem and the solution interact in many different types of tasks and contexts, they argue, they are quick to identify patterns and offer qualified suggestions for possible solu-tions to a wide and diverse range of problems. Cross describes this ability as an approach that is unique to designers but underscores that creative thinking is not some sort of 'mysterious' talent: it is essentially about letting the problem and the solution interact, and that ability comes with experience — what Cross refers to as the particular 'designerly way of knowing'.[45]

Cross's interest in designers' creativity is representative of the general focus in design studies on the cognitive aspects of design work and approaches that can be used to manage, direct or qualify design processes. However, it may seem odd that design cognition studies have not focused more on the material and form-related aspects that constitute the outcome of the design process, manifested as form, product or concept.

In relation to the general understandings of design thinking, the form aspects of design thinking could arguably be seen as the most privileged area for the trained designer. Thus, in agenda-setting management publications about design thinking, such as Richard Boland and Frank Collopy's *Managing as Designing* and Roberto Verganti's *Design-Driven Innovation*, it is the fascination with prominent architects and design products that drives the interest in exploring not only how designers think but also how they go about materialising concepts as sketches or tangible form. In its quest to understand designers' cognitive skills, design research related to the design field may have been blind to the particular qualities that have historically given the design profession its unique position in society. Here, design history research and studies of design culture — based mainly in the humanities and material culture studies — may have something to offer in terms of describing and evaluating the quality of the ultimate outcomes of design thinking: sketches, prototypes, spaces, products or material or immaterial concepts.

Artistic design thinking. In Denmark, the design programmes at the Royal Danish Academy of Fine Arts and Design School Kolding are defined by an explicitly artistic foundation. Thus, the programmes focus not only on design disciplines such as problem-solving and the formulation of proposals but also on the artistic qualities of the outcome and whether it contains qualities normally associated with a work of art: an aesthetic expression based on sensuous, tactile or emotional dimensions and/or inherent meaning or communicative aspects, based on its ability to reflect its core idea, for example by relating to itself in terms of genre, type or product. This implies an emphasis on material and conceptual aspects of design work with an interest in their ability to rise above the commonplace or bring a unique quality to their surroundings or the user situation, which is arguably the principal goal of the practice manifested in design thinking and design doing.

2.6.
Design and designerly thinking as a goal-driven or an explorative endeavour

The difference between the general and the professional approach to design thinking is reflected in the current focus in design thinking studies on how designers and practitioners of design thinking think and act in processes.

In this debate, there seem to be two basic positions in contemporary academic design thinking studies. One position considers design thinking as something that unfolds mainly in relation to a goal-driven act. Design is seen, above all, as a problem-solving activity aimed at achieving a desired or preferred state and typically realised in a material or immaterial solution. The process is largely informed by design briefs or demand specifications, which define the goal that informs the designer's or design team's work as they move through the various stages of the process. In terms of genre, we mainly see this position represented within the classic design disciplines, such as product design or graphic communication, where the work is often guided by a brief and aims to achieve a specific form or product.

The second position views design as primarily an inquiry-based activity that explores a task or a problem in depth without necessarily arriving at a final, materialised proposal for a solution.

The inquiry-based approach often aims at creating platforms for the development of processes or change, where different actors, including non-designers, can be engaged over time, typically in the form of new design approaches, such as co-design or co-creation, which use a variety of methods aimed at facilitating co-creative processes that involve the participation of users, citizens or other external stakeholders.

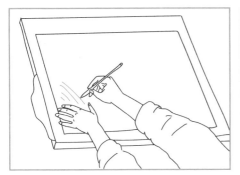

Brief-driven or explorative. Historically, trained designers have focused primarily on designing a solution based on a brief with certain demand specifications. Traditionally, the design competence has thus been focused on solving a problem and fulfilling the requests outlined in the brief, largely associated with form and often situated at the latter stages of a decision-making process. New design genres, such as co-design or co-creation, include multiple process stages, from problem or idea to prototype to solution. These new genres also represent a more explorative approach to design thinking that does not necessarily result in a design product. Instead, the outcome of the process may be a new concept for a service, a vision or a strategy, which is not necessarily realised as form.

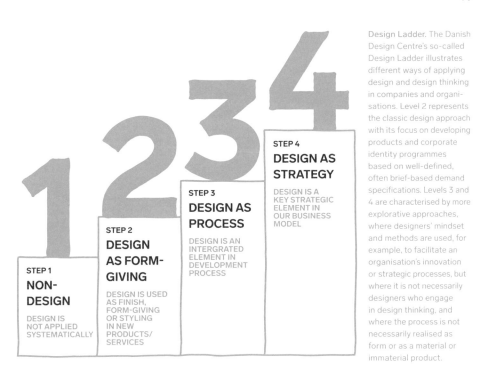

STEP 4

DESIGN AS STRATEGY

DESIGN IS A KEY STRATEGIC ELEMENT IN OUR BUSINESS MODEL

STEP 3

DESIGN AS PROCESS

DESIGN IS AN INTERGRATED ELEMENT IN DEVELOPMENT PROCESS

STEP 2

DESIGN AS FORM-GIVING

DESIGN IS USED AS FINISH, FORM-GIVING OR STYLING IN NEW PRODUCTS/SERVICES

STEP 1

NON-DESIGN

DESIGN IS NOT APPLIED SYSTEMATICALLY

Design Ladder. The Danish Design Centre's so-called Design Ladder illustrates different ways of applying design and design thinking in companies and organisations. Level 2 represents the classic design approach with its focus on developing products and corporate identity programmes based on well-defined, often brief-based demand specifications. Levels 3 and 4 are characterised by more explorative approaches, where designers' mindset and methods are used, for example, to facilitate an organisation's innovation or strategic processes, but where it is not necessarily designers who engage in design thinking, and where the process is not necessarily realised as form or as a material or immaterial product.

The explorative approaches to design thinking often include users or 'non-designers' throughout the design process, from the initial idea to the finished product. Thus also in the initial, so-called 'fuzzy front end', to quote the term coined by the design theorists Liz Sanders and Pieter Jan Stappers.[46] This is where the design problem is defined and understood, and where the designer and the users together can 'rehearse the future', to borrow the design theorist Joachim Halse's term, by proposing and testing different solutions and then implementing and evaluating them.[47] One example might be the development and testing of new waste-sorting facilities for multi-storey residential buildings, where prototypes for separate bins and the waste-handling company's collection procedures are developed in collaboration with stakeholders as 'act-it-out prototypes' that take form in a dialogue with an imagined practice.[48]

Rethinking Design Thinking. The innovation consultancy firm Humantific operates with four types of design thinking: 'Design & Design Thinking' 1.0 and 2.0 are characterised by the use of 'conventional design thinking methodologies' aimed at 'small-scale challenges' and are mainly brief-oriented, problem-solving and form-driven in their approach. 'Design & Design Thinking' 3.0 and 4.0 are focused on 'wicked problems', here intended to mean 'giant-scale challenges' at the level of systems, organisations, industries, community, country and planet. While methods have been developed for the first two levels over several years, Humantific points to the need for new methods for handling the giant-scale challenges on levels 3.0 and 4.0, where the traditional methods may often fall short.[49]

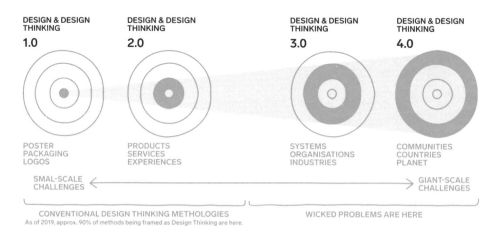

DESIGN & DESIGN THINKING

1.0

POSTER
PACKAGING
LOGOS

DESIGN & DESIGN THINKING

2.0

PRODUCTS
SERVICES
EXPERIENCES

DESIGN & DESIGN THINKING

3.0

SYSTEMS
ORGANISATIONS
INDUSTRIES

DESIGN & DESIGN THINKING

4.0

COMMUNITIES
COUNTRIES
PLANET

SMAL-SCALE
CHALLENGES ←   → GIANT-SCALE
CHALLENGES

CONVENTIONAL DESIGN THINKING METHOLOGIES
As of 2019, approx. 90% of methods being framed as Design Thinking are here.

WICKED PROBLEMS ARE HERE

DESIGN PHILOSOPHY
Many Design & Design Thinking philosophies reflect intention to span this terrain from Design 1.0 to 4.0

By contrast, more traditional approaches typically place the main emphasis on conceptualising and prototyping approaches. This is where the idea or design concept is developed, where the form is determined, and thus where the classic design competence resides. In form-driven processes, the users are typically only included at much later stages to evaluate whether the prototype needs adjusting. The classic approaches to the design process are sometimes criticised for not being sufficiently user-centred. Within new fields, such as design-driven innovation (see p. 60), the assumption is that 'designers know best', because their creativity and sensibility to, for example, the cultural context and the spirit of the times, enable them to come up with unexpected solutions that the users did not know they needed. Their artistic talent and aesthetic competence, further, enable them to propose novel solutions that rise above the mundane or average.

One criticism of explorative design thinking, on the other hand, has been that it often struggles to get past the exploration stage because it can be both costly and cumbersome to include users at every stage of the process. Hence, the proposed solutions may simply be in the form of the much-maligned Post-it notes on a board, an outcome that does not in itself lead to concrete products or promote the desired changes.[50]

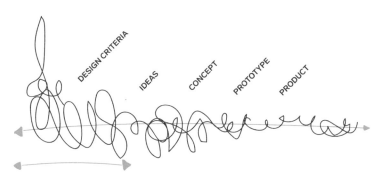

DESIGN CRITERIA

IDEAS

CONCEPT

PROTOTYPE

PRODUCT

FUZZY FRONT END

Fuzzy Front End. Design researchers Lis Sanders and Pieter Jan Stappers illustrate the so-called front-end phase of design development as a complex process that begins with confusion and complexity and then progresses towards ever greater clarity. The idea behind co-design is that coming users – so-called non-designers – are included at every stage of the process, in contrast to, for example, the classic brief-driven design approaches, which are mainly focused on the phases that Sanders and Stappers call ideas, concept and prototype.[51]

Riding the coat-tails of the users. In user-driven design approaches, which are represented in participatory design or co-design, among other fields, the users are ideally included at every stage of the process, from the initial idea to the finished result. Unlike the classic approaches to design development, where the brief is typically defined by a client or conceived by the designer as an idea for solving a problem, user-driven approaches also engage the users in identifying or coming up with the problem to be addressed. One example might be a manufacturer of sports attire who wishes to explore unmet needs among extreme-sports athletes. In this case, the first stage of the process would typically consist of ethnographically oriented studies of the athletes, including their behaviour, values, equipment and ways of socialising. The process would include talks about what they might imagine could be different, for example improved activities or experiences. This exploration would typically consist of what-if scenarios: 'What if we did it this way? How would that affect the activity?' This approach thus examines both problems and possibilities in a collaborative process.

In the long run — and justifiably so — simplistic, easy-to-follow design thinking approaches risk criticism because they, naturally, fail to deliver as promised. That presents a challenge to the deep design professionalism that the academically anchored design thinking represents. It is important to be aware that design thinking is always followed by hard work when it comes to implementing the solutions: 'after the ecstasy, the laundry.' It takes major resources to carry out user-involving processes, and there are no quick fixes, contrary to the impression one might gain from IDEO's and some of Stanford University's versions of design thinking.

2.7.
Design and designerly thinking as a science of the imaginary

Recent design thinking studies speak of design thinking as a science of the imaginary. In this understanding, the idea is that design research only takes place through practice,[52] as the researcher develops proposals for new realities that are brought to life, for example, through prototypes, mock-ups and scenarios. This approach builds on those branches of design studies that are also called 'practice-based design research' or 'research through design' and which, in addition to requiring knowledge production, also contain an experimental or form-related practice.

With the purpose of developing the notion of a science of the imaginary, the design researchers Ilpo Koskinen, John Zimmerman, Thomas Binder, Johan Redström and Stephan Wensveen have proposed a new concept of a concretising and materialising form of design research, labelled 'Constructive Design Research'. Here, the construction itself — in the form of, for example, products, systems, spaces or media — is the key focus of knowledge production. It involves imagining and building something new, such as prototypes, mock-ups, scenarios or detailed concepts, and then sharing the knowledge that is generated through the process. [53]

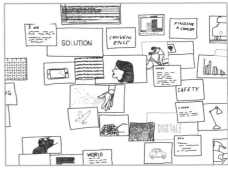

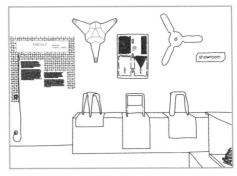

Laboratories, fieldwork and showrooms. Constructive design research typically derives insights through labs and fieldwork and demonstrates its knowledge through the so-called showroom. With inspiration from natural science, the lab is a place where things or challenges can be addressed and subjected to experiments in isolation from their ordinary context. Fieldwork is inspired by ethnography, where practices or issues are observed in their natural context. In the showroom, design results are presented, for example in the form of prototypes, scenarios or detailed concepts with a view to knowledge sharing.

Much of this constructive design research takes place in a dialogue
with non-designers who take part in the process of imagining
new things and realities and then, to the extent it is possible,
in developing and testing prototypes. The methods are related
to co-design, which also requires an 'open design', where the
everyman can, in principle, be an active participant. The process is
not only driven by an interest in sharing the form that the designer
establishes but treats the 'social' aspects — the participants'
experiences, everyday knowledge and concrete challenges — as
equally important parts of the design material as the material or
immaterial form resulting from the process. [54]

The constructive approach to design
thinking, including the related fields of
co-design and participatory design, have
been criticised for favouring processes
and prototypes over the finished result
and thus failing to consider the quality
of the outcome. This involves a risk that
the designer's role is defined purely as
that of a facilitator, which means that the
aspects of form and aesthetics are given
a lower priority.[55]

2.8.
Design and designerly thinking as serendipity

The design researcher Gabriela Goldschmidt, who, like Cross and Lawson, among others, bases her research on observation studies of designers, has determined that sketches and other types of visual materials are the most important tools for facilitating the open-ended and explorative nature of the design activity. She speaks of design competence as a *visual* form of knowledge, which means that the designer has a so-called prepared eye.[56]

In the design practice, according to Goldschmidt, the design practitioner has to be able to engage in a search that is not specifically goal-driven. To develop that capacity, designers must have a 'prepared eye' that is able to take advantage of the stimuli it encounters, randomly or intentionally. Moreover, naturally, in the concretisation stage, the designer also needs to recognise the right solution once it presents itself.[57] In Goldschmidt's understanding, sketching and prototyping may be the trained designer's most important tools. They are the processes that give the ideas shape, and they involve both the reflective eye and the trained hand.

In the mid 18th century, Immanuel Kant wrote that 'The hand is the window to the mind', which can also be seen as a core notion in design thinking, where the hand, the sketch and physical sensation are all closely related to reflection.[58] A propositional, synthesising mindset is a condition for generating novel and innovative solutions to tasks and problems. Through their training, designers develop a trained eye and hand and also gain access to a historical and cultural reservoir of knowledge. In combination with a talent for drawing or shaping solutions in many different types of materials and technologies, this builds a capacity for both divergent and convergent thinking that promotes creativity and, ultimately, enables designers to bring a particular materialised, sensuous or aesthetic quality to concepts and objects.

This practice is not something that can be acquired in a brief training course in design thinking. According to the philosopher Richard Sennett, it takes 10,000 hours (or about 20 hours a week for 10 years) to become an expert.[59] Thus, it is not possible to become a concert pianist by taking piano lessons once a week. Similarly, one does not become a professional design thinker by learning a simple just-follow-the-steps method. On the other hand, weekly lessons can make you a passable piano player, which can be a fine platform for understanding and appreciating the true mastery of the professional pianist. The same applies to design thinking: there are professional practitioners, most of them trained designers with years of experience, and amateurs who may have a keen interest but limited skill, because they lack experience: cognitive 'knowledge in practice', a prepared eye and trained hand.

The concept of serendipity may touch on the core of design thinking related to the design field, which deals with designers' creativity based on their prepared eye and trained hand and their ability to engage in both divergent and convergent thinking. Together, these qualities enable them to give their ideas shape.

2.9.
Design and designerly thinking as a path to sensemaking

One aspect of designers' visual and tactile training is the development of an understanding of the cultural context that designers create designs to fit into and function in. To understand how design can be conceived in a dialogue with its cultural context we may turn to so-called product semantics, a field of study that originated at the Hochschule für Gestaltung in Ulm, and which offers a semantic understanding of design thinking studies that relate to design practice. During the 1950s, product semantics studied how products, interfaces and visual forms might communicate meaning in different contexts.

A key figure in this field is the design theorist Klaus Krippendorff, who trained at the Ulm School, and who has analysed how designers address meaning and sensemaking in product development. In his 2006 book *The Semantic Turn* Krippendorff proposes a 'semantic turn' in design: a shift in focus for designers from the functional dimensions of design products to the attri- butions of meaning that they are subjected to in their respective contexts. It is Krippendorff's point that design practitioners need to be able to understand and address these attributions in their work. In summarising his point, Krippendorff rephrases the architect Louis Sullivan's famous dictum 'form follows function' as 'form follows meaning'. In Krippendorff's understanding, 'meaning' refers to the meaning that is created for and by the user when a 'form' is put to use.[60]

> While Goldschmidt speaks of the prepared eye, Krippendorff sees design practice as an endeavour to understand and produce cultural meaning contexts for design. For the trained designer, this is obviously understood to take place at an advanced level, although a wide variety of professions, according to Krippendorff, can benefit from working with design semantics.

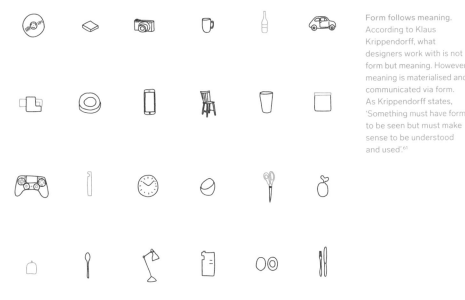

Form follows meaning. According to Klaus Krippendorff, what designers work with is not form but meaning. However, meaning is materialised and communicated via form. As Krippendorff states, 'Something must have form to be seen but must make sense to be understood and used'.[61]

In his book *Design-Driven Innovation. Changing the rules of competition by radically innovating what things mean* (2009) the innovation and management scholar Roberto Verganti introduces Krippendorff's work in a marketing-focused innovation context. He argues that 'innovation in meaning' is just as important as technological innovation, although the latter is the primary focus in the innovation literature.[62] One of Verganti's examples is the Italian design firm Alessi, whose kitchen products introduced what Verganti calls 'a radical new meaning' in everyday objects such as corkscrews and citrus squeezers. The products stand out by not only communicating their function but also containing a dimension of meaning that can be subjected to various cultural or symbolic interpretations.

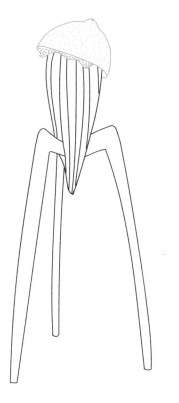

Design-driven innovation. According to Roberto Verganti, Philip Starck's famous citrus squeezer is an example of design-driven innovation that springs from designers' ability to give products a new meaning. In this case, the citrus squeezer not only communicates its function but also appeals to our imagination and is the object of various attributions of meaning.

One of Verganti's key points is that designers have a particular ability to understand and work with cultural contexts, because they possess a sensibility that enables them to sense new trends long before they are manifested in the market, for example. Rather than relying on consumers, for example by undertaking costly consumer and market surveys, Verganti recommends an approach based on 'design-driven innovation', where companies either hire in-house designers or work with a network of designers as a way of driving innovation in their company.

Verganti's recommendation of 'design-driven innovation' is a rejection of the tendency for uniformity and the lack of radical innovation in companies. However, the emphasis on a design-driven approach has also raised questions about when it makes sense to include users and about the scope and timing of user involvement in the process. These questions are also relevant for design fields such as co-design and participatory design, which ideally require user involvement in some or all of the stages of a design process but which are costly and resource-intensive. Thus, it is important to consider whether the approach actually leads to superior or more innovative solutions.

Design semantics is a promising approach to design thinking that may facilitate more expansive discussions of the unique abilities of trained designers. It involves not only making proposals but also doing so in an unorthodox way and with results that give our products and surroundings a unique or added quality. These are dimensions that can be categorised as 'aesthetic', which in relation to design involves considering the different ways in which objects, products, spaces and interactions speak to us and seek to appear attractive or to challenge our senses and our understanding.

As outlined in this chapter, design and designerly thinking represent a multidisciplinary field spanning multiple theoretical positions and a wide variety of topics, methodological practices and ideas about what the thinking can and should result in. In the following, we turn to the management discourse on design thinking. This is a younger field with a less complete theoretical basis than the research-based design studies, but it has been more successful at positioning itself in the general public and has thus made a significant contribution to the growing interest in design thinking across a growing number of industries and sectors.

Design-driven innovation. Design thinking does not need to involve users but may be manifested as so-called design-driven innovation. According to innovation theorists such as Roberto Verganti, the latter involves an inside-out approach. Rather than listening to what the users want, designers listen instead to the particular sensibility designers and artists possess, including a sensitivity to trends. A design-driven approach assumes that companies are able to offer consumers what they did not know they wanted, and in some cases, that has a far greater innovative potential than user involvement — a point that Henry Ford also confidently made: 'If I had asked people what they wanted, they would have said faster horses.'

Chapter 3
Management discourses about design thinking

What characterises management discourses about design thinking is that design competences are being applied outside a traditional design context and with a primary emphasis on management and organisational development.[63]

In the following we focus on four sub-discourses, based in part on Johansson-Sköldberg et al.'s distinction, supplemented with more detailed descriptions of the professional or disciplinary orientation of the approaches and the agenda-setting publications that reflect them.

3.1.
Design thinking as design management

The first sub-discourse that we will examine could be called 'design thinking as design management'. This approach could, in principle, be considered part of those areas of design research I have categorised under 'design and designerly thinking discourses', as it has its origins in the design studies related to design practice, while the following three sub-discourses are rooted in more traditional management studies.

Design thinking as design management originated from the design method research that emerged during the 1960s. During the 1970s, as part of the design method studies, an interest emerged in how designers' methods can be used as a management tool at different organisational levels. In 1975, this led to the establishment of the Design Management Institute (DMI) at Massachusetts College of Art in Boston and in 1989, to the launch of the *Design Management Review*, a magazine that further helped manifest design management as an independent discipline.

Historically, design management has roots in the fields of corporate identity and corporate design, which emerged during the early 20th century represented by designer Peter Behrens's work for AEG and, later, Marcello Nizzoli's for Olivetti, among others. As the first 'chief designers' in history, they developed comprehensive programmes for the two companies' visual identity, thus making design a strategic management tool for the organisation's product and identity development, later known as branding.

Until the early 2000s, the field of design management was thus applied mainly in the development of products and corporate identity programmes. With the growing interest in design methods in recent years, the focus has expanded to include studies of how trained designers can play a role at a managerial level in industries outside the traditional design field.[64]

It is symptomatic that the studies are focused mainly on how business managers can learn from how designers think and work. Design management publications such as Rachel Cooper & Jürgen Faust (2011); Junginger et. al. (2016), Nussbaum (2013), among others, have introduced design methods for use in management and strategic corporate development and thus invited business managers into the designers' domain with the professional — perhaps even ideological — objective of bringing designers into the executive domain.

In recent years, the field of design management has generated a growing number of articles and books discussing how designers' methods and traditional management approaches can be combined with the dual goal of giving management a more innovative edge and including design as a strategic executive tool. The latter is to be achieved either by including designers at the table when strategic decisions are made or by including them as external consultants to advise management.

DESIGN FOCUS

	STRATEGY	EXPERIENCE	SERVICES	SYSTEMS	PRODUCTS
CUSTOMER SEGMENTS					
VALUE PROPOSITIONS					
CUSTOMER RELATIONS					
CHANNELS					
KEY ACTIVITIES					
KEY RESOURCES					
KEY PARTNERS					

SUBJECT

The strategic design matrix developed by Jørgen Rasmussen et al. (2012) proposes a combination of business and design thinking. The subject focus of the model is represented by a terminology drawn from Alexander Osterwalder's Business Model Canvas. The 'design focus' axis is inspired by John Heskett's model of design practice (2005), which ranges from products to systems, services, experiences and strategic development. The purpose of the matrix is to help corporate managers and employees identify possible focus areas and to take a strategic approach to the development potential.

Recipe for design thinking. According to Liedtka and Ogilvie (2012), design thinking can be put in a simple formula. With inspiration from cookbooks, which offer easy-to-follow recipes, a simple recipe aims to make it easy to combine business and design thinking. A four-stage approach helps combine the analytic thinking from business, which aims to analyse existing value chains, with the prototyping, visualising and explorative approaches that characterise design thinking.

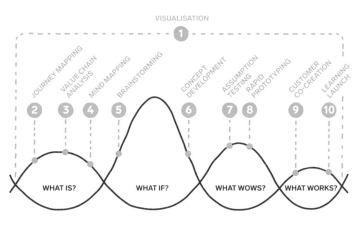

One example of the publications that combine traditional management tools with the designer's prototyping approach is the article 'Prototyping Design and Business' by the design researchers Jørgen Rasmussen, Gunnar Kramp and Bo Mortensen (2012). The article introduces a matrix specifying management tools based on mercantile, prototyping and design thinking approaches with 35 focus areas intended for the development of strategies, products and services.

Similarly, in the article 'Helping Business Managers Discover their Appetite for Design Thinking', the design management thinkers Jeanne Liedtka and Tim Ogilvie (2012) present a tool for business managers who want to work at the intersection of design and business. The article is based on the notion that working with design thinking should be straightforward. With inspiration from Julia Child's famous cookbook *Mastering the Art of French Cooking* from 1961, which fostered widespread international interest in French cuisine by providing detailed recipes, Liedtka and Ogilvie propose a model consisting of four basic questions: 'What Is?', 'What If?', 'What Wows?', 'What Works?' The questions are addressed by means of specific tools focusing on analysis, prototyping and evaluation. In contrast to Rasmussen et al.'s article, which is based on research within both design and business, Leidker and Ogilvie's article is an example of the many practice-based 'recipes' that have appeared in recent years in step with the growing interest in design thinking within management and which have given the impression that design thinking is 'easy to learn'.

A point of debate in design management studies has been whether trained designers can or should be involved at a strategic level in companies and, if so, how? A related topic of discussion has been whether it is not 'good enough' if managers or CEOs have knowledge and awareness of the value of design and are able to bring it into the executive suite as a competence, for example on a consultancy basis, based on the idea that managers are better at managing, while designers are better at designing and engaging in professional design thinking.

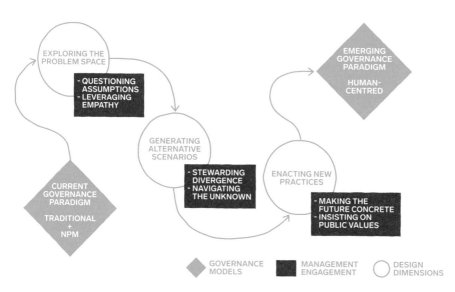

Changing governance by design. Based on a number of case studies in public-sector companies in a range of countries including Denmark, England, Finland and the United States, Bason (2012) proposes a conceptual framework for both a current and an emerging paradigm of public governance. The left side of the figure shows the so-called traditional governance and new public management paradigms, while the right side shows a possible governance model based on three main stages: exploring the problem space, generating alternative scenarios and enacting new practices. Each of the three stages is associated with several possible design engagements for public managers.[65]

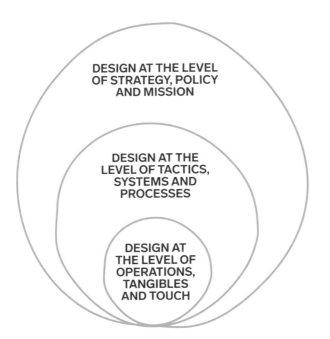

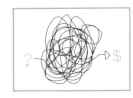

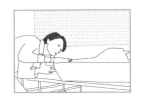

Levels of design management. Design management studies have emerged from design method research and rest on a fundamental notion that trained designers can take on managerial roles on several organisational levels: from the product-oriented, tactile level, where design is a tool for product development; to the tactical levels, where design approaches are a tool for project management or process facilitation aimed, for example, at stimulating innovation and creative methods – typically in mid-level management; to strategic levels, where design thinking can be used as a tool to develop new business models and visions for companies.[66]

One example of an extensive study of the use of design management thinking in organisational development is the Danish design researcher and CEO of the Danish Design Centre, Christian Bason's visionary PhD dissertation *Leading Public Design. How Managers Engage with Design to Transform Public Governance*, which focuses on the use of design management in the public sector. The dissertation is based on 15 case studies across five countries and examines how public-sector managers view and apply design tools as well as the potential of design to be a catalyst of change in public organisations and on a political governance level. Based on the case studies, Bason proposes a model for possible design contributions to traditional management and governance paradigms, where designers' methods supplement the established management models with a more explorative and prototyping mindset.

3.2.
Design thinking as synonymous with IDEO's approach

In the management-oriented discourses, the design consultancy firm IDEO is probably the most influential voice due to its international success, promoted in part by bestseller publications, consultancy work for global brands and close collaboration with Stanford University.

Initially, IDEO's version of design thinking was mainly communicated by the people involved in the company. Since then, it has circulated in countless incarnations in a growing number of articles, blogs and consultancies that are inspired by IDEO and which have thus contributed to a wider promotion of the company's methods.

According to the company's own historiography, David Kelley, the founder of IDEO and a professor at Stanford University, invented design thinking in the early 2000s as a new concept for the firm, which had existed since 1991 with a main focus on product development. In an interview from 2009, Brown describes it almost as a case of mystical inspiration: 'In a meeting with IDEO's CEO, Tim Brown, in 2003, Kelley had an epiphany: They would stop calling IDEO's approach "design" and start calling it "design thinking". "I'm not a words person," Kelley says, "but in my life, it's the most powerful moment that words or labeling ever made. Because then it all made sense. Now I'm an expert at methodology rather than a guy who designs a new chair or car.'[67]

The idea of making design thinking the centre of IDEO's services was a natural continuation of the firm's focus on creativity in its consultancy work. The concept was promoted in books such as *The Art of Innovation: Lessons in Creativity from IDEO, America's Leading Design Firm* (2001) and *The Ten Faces of Innovation and IDEO's Strategies for Beating the Devil's Advocate and Driving Creativity Throughout Your Organization* (2005), both written by Tom Kelley, David Kelley's brother and the CEO of IDEO. In the books, IDEO is marketed as the creative watchdog of management consultancy, illustratively exemplified with case stories about the companies and global brands IDEO has helped become more innovative in their business development.

A persistent theme in IDEO's version of design thinking is that it is not a professional competence that is unique to trained designers but an approach that anyone, in principle, can learn. In a slightly clichéd comment on designers, IDEO's CEO, Tim Brown, states, 'Contrary to popular opinion, you don't need weird shoes or a black turtleneck to be a design thinker. Nor are design thinkers necessarily created only by design schools, even though most professionals have some kind of design training. My experience is that many people outside professional design have a natural aptitude for design thinking, which the right development and experience can unlock.'[68]

With this view of design thinking, Brown contributes to the widespread perception of design thinking as an activity that people of all professional background can engage in. In 2008, Brown wrote the widely quoted article 'Design Thinking' in *Harvard Business Review*, which introduces design thinking as a method invented by IDEO, again with illustrative examples of business and healthcare organisations that IDEO advised on management and organisational development.

In what is often described as the most widely quoted article on design thinking, the concept is presented as a simple method that may serve as inspiration to any company.[69] Symptomatically of IDEO's communication style, it is described as a straightforward approach consisting of three simple steps: 'inspiration', 'ideation' and 'implementation'.[70] The inspiration stage is an open-ended process aimed at discovering new possibilities for the company to act and operate in the marketplace. Ideation is about exploring possibilities and testing proposals before the chosen solution is implemented in the organisation. According to Brown, the unique quality of the method is its strong focus on inspiration and ideation, where executives and employees can be inspired by designers' sensibility, method and process repertoire and thus infuse more creativity into their working methods and organisational development.

INSPIRATION

THE PROBLEM OR
OPPORTUNITY THAT
MOTIVATES THE SEARCH
FOR SOLUTIONS

IDEATION

THE PROCESS OF GENER-
ATING, DEVELOPING, AND
TESTING IDEAS

IMPLEMENTATION

THE PATH THAT LEADS
FROM THE PROJECT STAGE
INTO PEOPLE'S LIVES

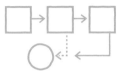

Inspiration, ideation, implementation. According to Brown, design thinking is 'a discipline that uses the designer's sensibility and methods to match people's needs with what is technologically feasible and what a viable business strategy can convert into customer value and market opportunity'.⁷¹ The three-stage model of inspiration, ideation and implementation can, in principle, be learned and practised by anyone and does not require design training.

In 2009, the article was followed up by Brown's bestselling book *Change by Design. How Design Thinking Transforms Organizations and Inspires Innovation* (published in a revised edition in 2019), which describes IDEO's use of design thinking and underscores that it is a method that is accessible to a wide range of professions. In 2015, *Havard Business Review* published two new articles by Brown. The first, 'When Everyone is Doing Design Thinking Is It Still a Competitive Advantage?', reviews design thinking six years after the first article was published. It reiterates the point that all organisations can still learn from design thinking, but it also makes a new point: that it is a discipline that requires training and experience. The second article, 'Design for Action', co-authored with Roger Martin, positions IDEO as part of a broader historical development of the design discipline. In this article, Simon and Buchanan are credited as seminal contributors in the development of design thinking, and IDEO is described as the company that popularised the approach. Like IDEO's other publications, it presents a number of cases and makes repeated references to IDEO as a consultancy or educational framework for design thinking.

A characteristic of the publications from IDEO is that they are written as practice-based how-to-oriented instructions featuring illustrative examples showing how IDEO has helped the company's clients adopt a more innovative approach to organisational, service or business development and how the firm's courses in collaboration with Stanford University, among others, have trained executives and staff to think like designers. Undoubtedly, the broad communication strategy, the influential role of IDEO's successful consultants and, not least, David Kelley's dual role as the founder of IDEO and a professor at Stanford University contributed to the spread of IDEO's methods within a wide range of sectors that had not necessarily been practising design or design thinking. However, some critics find that IDEO has been capitalising on designers' mindset and methods with a fairly clichéd representation of designers and also, in many of the early publications, failing to familiarise itself with and referring to the years-long studies of design thinking in theory and practice within the design profession.[72]

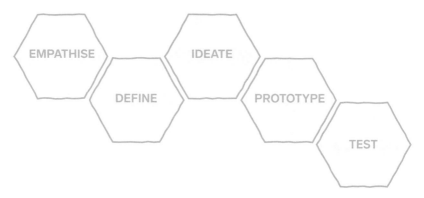

Empathy. Brown's three-stage model from 2008 was subsequently modified, and several versions have been proposed, including the model above, where the original three stages have been supplemented with the front-end stage of 'empathy', while the other four stages are labelled 'define', 'ideate', 'prototype' and 'test'. The model has been depicted in a variety of ways. In a reflection of the dynamic character of the design process, the model above represents the stages as building blocks that can be combined in different ways, depending on the given context or situation. Due in part to Kelley's dual role as professor at Stanford University and the founder of IDEO, the model has also been promoted via Stanford University's commercial courses on design thinking and is generally known as the IDEO/Stanford method.

3.3.
Design thinking as an approach to complex organisational problems

A related management approach has been proposed by Roger Martin, the former dean of the Rothmann School of Business at Toronto University. In his book *The Design of Business: Why Design Thinking is the Next Competitive Advantage* (2009) Martin presents a vision of making executives and companies more innovative by not focusing exclusively on analytical thinking but instead balancing the left and right brain hemispheres by means of design thinking, which he introduces as a concept of his own invention: 'The most successful businesses in the years to come will balance analytical mastery and intuitive originality in a dynamic interplay that I call design thinking.'[73]

In the book Martin backs away from his own previous call for the need for more analytical thinking in corporate management. Among other influences, he points to his collaboration with IDEO as a key cause of his discovery of the value of creative thinking in corporate management.[74] In the book, design thinking is defined as 'A person or organisation (...) constantly seeking a fruitful balance between reliability and validity, between art and science, between intuition and analytics, and between exploration and exploitation'. These are qualities that, according to Martin, are associated with the designer's most important tool, 'abductive thinking', which Martin considers an important supplement to analytical thinking.[75]

According to Martin, all companies have the potential to become 'design thinking firms', just as we all have the potential to become 'design thinkers'. A design thinker is defined as a 'first-class-noticer'[76] and design thinking firms as 'world-class explorers', which — importantly — have to be willing to give up their traditional ways of leading and handling processes in order to reap the benefits of design thinking.[77] In line with Kelley's and Brown's writings, Martin presents examples of companies that have introduced design thinking and of how the new management approach has led to greater innovation and economic growth, albeit without documenting or substantiating these claims in any detail.

Similarly, Martin introduces specific methods that executives can use in practice. Design thinking is described as a simple procedure consisting of an iterative cycle of idea generation (abduction), prediction of consequences (deduction), testing and generalisation (induction). Further, Martin suggests that design thinking should be included in strategic executive processes as part of the so-called knowledge funnel where complex organisational issues are handled through ideation and the establishment of viable practices and guidelines framing the company's operations and development.

Martin has been criticised for prioritising focus and regularity at the cost of eliminating the messy and unpredictable qualities from design thinking. His 'knowledge funnel' reflects a fundamentally linear mindset where it is only at the first stage that executives and employees are allowed to be in the unknown and play at being designers. On the other hand, this linear mindset might be precisely what made Martin's messages of design thinking acceptable in management circles.

THE KNOWLEDGE FUNNEL

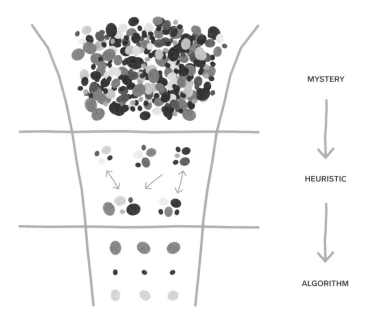

MYSTERY

HEURISTIC

ALGORITHM

Design thinking in the knowledge funnel. In Roger Martin's book *The Design of Business* (2009) design thinking is introduced as a new element to be included in the so-called knowledge funnel guiding executives' strategic processes aimed at generating new knowledge to promote innovation. The funnel has three stages: a 'mystery' stage where the unsolved problems are explored; a 'heuristic' stage, where guidelines and practices begin to take form and become what Martin calls rules of thumb; and an 'algorithm' stage which results in a robust business offering. One example might be the fast-food logistics applied by McDonald's. Martin says that most companies tend to operate at the two lower stages of the funnel. However, if executives wish to move their companies in a more innovative direction they have to learn to spend longer at the first stage of the funnel, and they have to be willing to return to it several times during an innovation process.

Martin's enthusiasm for design thinking also sparked an interest in introducing design thinking in business management training. Martin has pioneered this development with articles in *Academy of Management Learning & Education*, including his agenda-setting interview with David Dunne, 'Design Thinking and How It Will Change Management Education: An Interview and Discussion' (2006), which has been followed up with several articles in management journals about how design thinking can contribute to business management education.[78]

IDEO's and Martin's introduction of design thinking in management contexts undoubtedly played an important role in the spread of designers' thinking and practice outside traditional design contexts. Martin's influence as dean of the Rothmann School of Business and as a management consultant to some of the world's biggest international corporations put him at the top of Forbes's 2017 list of the most influential business thinkers. In combination with IDEO's international success this has contributed to the global spread of IDEO's and Martin's versions of design thinking. In several popular publications design thinking is presented as synonymous with IDEO's and Martin's approaches.[79]

In comparison to deep, multifaceted studies of how designers approach design thinking within the design profession, IDEO's and Martin's presentations may seem a little shallow. It is also remarkable that the writers present design thinking as a self-invented concept, seemingly unaware of the large body of research literature on design cognition that has developed since the 1960s.

In 2018, Martin's colleague David Dunne's book *Design Thinking at Work. How Organizations Are Embracing Design* came out. Like Brown's and Martin's *Havard Business Review* articles from 2015 the book challenges the stereotypical image of design thinking as something anyone can easily learn to master. In line with earlier titles by Martin and Dunne, the book focuses on how companies can approach complex organisational problems by means of design thinking. However, as a new feature it also incorporates the academic literature on design thinking, which thus frames the empirical studies of governments, multinational corporations and non-profit organisations that have used design thinking. With this, the book marks a break with the management literature's earlier celebration of design thinking as a quick-fix solution and a move towards more in-depth analyses of the challenges associated with implementing design thinking as an established approach in the organisation.

In combination with meta-studies by Kimbell, Johansson-Sköldberg et al. and others, Dunne's book and the growing flow of articles on design thinking in management education can hopefully contribute to greater perspective, deeper insight and increased dialogue among the different versions of design thinking.

3.4.
Design thinking as part of management and innovation theory

A fourth approach to design thinking within the management field was introduced by the management theorists Richard Boland and Frank Collopy, whose anthology *Managing as Designing* (2004) proposes a change in management practice and education with inspiration from the creativity offered by design thinking. The anthology was compiled in extension of a workshop in connection with the official opening of Frank Gehry's Weatherhead School of Management in Cleveland, Ohio, and with explicit inspiration from Gehry's approach.[80]

The purpose of the anthology was to initiate a professional debate about where design thinking can be integrated as part of management theory. However, only three of the contributors come from a design research background: Buchanan, Jürgen Faust and Ilya Prokopoff. The others have backgrounds within management, sociology, economics and music, among other fields.

In the introduction to the anthology, Boland and Collopy refer to Simon's definition of design as an endeavour aimed at 'changing existing situations into preferred ones', and in the book they further draw parallels between management and design by pointing to the challenges that managers and designers share, as they see it.[81] For example, both designers and managers often find themselves in situations that are not of their own making but where they are, nevertheless, responsible for finding solutions and achieving a desirable outcome. Moreover, both groups work with a problem space that does not afford clear-cut criteria for judging one solution in comparison with another, yet they must develop proposals and offer solutions.[82]

In the anthology, Boland and Collopy treat 'design thinking' as synonymous with 'design attitude' (the expectations and orientations one brings into a project). Thus, they describe design less as a way of working or as a working process with certain specific characteristics (as in IDEO's version, for example) and more as an activity defined by the cognitive characteristics of management that Martin is also interested in.[83] If there is a common frame of reference for the contributions to the anthology, it is Simon's definition of design as an endeavour 'aimed at changing existing situations into preferred ones'. As Johansson-Sköldberg et al. have pointed out in a critique of the book, however, the wide range of well-known scholars from other fields seem merely to use the design situation as an occasion to describe their own fields' frameworks of thinking and theory.

Several influential anthologies on design thinking published by Stanford University and the Hasso Plattner Research Foundation can also be seen as part of this understanding. Remarkably, however, they are not mentioned by Johansson-Sköldberg et al. or Kimbell. The HPI-Stanford Design Thinking Research Program was established in 2008, and in 2011, the first HPI anthology was published, initiating a series of yearbooks under the common title *Understanding Innovation*. The goal is to document the research that is conducted in the HPI programme, representing a context of engineering, management and innovation research. The research involves evidence- and case-based studies aimed at investigating design thinking as a phenomenon in its various contexts of technology, innovation and business development.[84] In accordance with the practice-oriented perspective of the books, the overriding purpose is to document frameworks, approaches and methods that have proved successful as well as identifying the challenges associated with the application of design thinking.[85] To that end, the books draw on both traditional design methodology research and empirical studies of the use of various types of design thinking methods in combination with approaches from management and innovation studies. The yearbooks document different perspectives on the use of design thinking, including studies of frameworks, tools and challenges in so-called creative design innovation (Plattner, Meinel & Leifer, 2011); co-creation as part of design thinking practice (2012a); innovation performance in design teams (2012b); possibilities and challenges in building innovation ecosystems (Leifer et al., 2014); and innovation teams (Plattner et al., 2015); studies and documentations of tools for enhancing creative interaction in innovation teams (2016a); studying wicked problems in complex areas with particular focus on IT systems engineering fields (2016b); design thinking as a tool for collaboration with a focus on education and training in design thinking (2018); success factors in design thinking in relation to digital technologies and solutions for complex challenges in the healthcare sector (Meinel & Leifer, 2019); and design thinking as a tool for leading cultural transformation in organisations with a focus on stimulating innovation (Ney & Meinel, 2019).

Design thinking as part of management and innovation theory. The businessman Hasso Plattner funded the establishment of the ambitious d.school programmes at Stanford University and Potsdam University. The HPI-Stanford Design Thinking Research Program was founded in 2008, and since 2011, it has published about a dozen yearbooks documenting the programme's studies in design thinking in various management, innovation and technology development contexts.

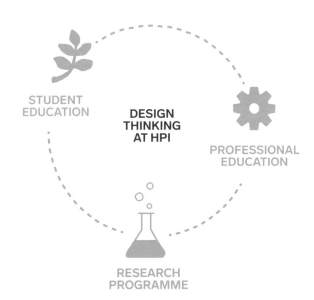

STUDENT EDUCATION

DESIGN THINKING AT HPI

PROFESSIONAL EDUCATION

RESEARCH PROGRAMME

The topics listed above demonstrate the wide range of the publications as well as a general orientation towards management and innovation development with a primary focus on technology development practices. A characteristic feature of the anthologies is the wide range of disciplines and professions that are involved in design thinking practice and research and a basic premise that 1) design thinking is a cross-disciplinary field that is not the exclusive reserve of designers, and 2) design thinking is a competence that requires training, education and, not least, input from cross-disciplinary research in design thinking.

In summary, the publications from the HPI Foundation represent a new level of research depth within the management approach to design thinking, which investigates and documents an expanded use of design thinking in the contexts of organisational and business development and which offers a diverse range of design thinking approaches as part of management and innovation theory. Moreover, the yearbooks contribute to more diverse understandings of the phenomenon of design thinking, which only underscores the need for dialogue among the many different understandings and approaches.

Several design researchers have criticised the management understandings of design thinking for treating it as synonymous with creativity and, in the popular versions, as a simplistic way of promoting creative thinking in management. However, creativity is only one aspect of the competences and practices that characterise the professional designer's work. Another point of criticism is that it often portrays design thinking as a simple toolbox, for example in the IDEO version's 'just-follow-the-steps' approach, which removes the designer's methods from their professional context and puts them on a simplistic 'ready-to-use' formula.[86] Since 2011, the HPI-Stanford Design Thinking Research Program has helped put the criticism of the quick-fix solutions to shame with a strong research and publishing practice that investigates the phenomenon of design thinking from different perspectives and in different contexts of technology, innovation and business development.

Chapter 4
Summary of design thinking discourses and a call to action

The following is an overview of design thinking and some of the key figures who shaped the field.

The model below offers an overview of the main fields of design thinking that were discussed in Chapters 2 and 3. The 'design and designerly thinking discourses' is further divided into a practice-oriented and a theoretical discourse. The practice-oriented understanding is labelled 'design thinking as a cognitive style' and is defined by a primary focus on empirical studies of how practising designers think and work. The theoretical understanding, which is labelled 'design thinking as a general theory of design', is characterised by a focus on investigating the scientific-theoretical basis of design as a discipline. The management understandings are divided into four fields: design thinking as design management; design thinking as synonymous with IDEO; design thinking as an approach to organisational problems; design thinking as part of management and innovation theory.

DESIGN AND DESIGNERLY THINKING DISCOURCES		MANAGEMENT DISCOURSES ABOUT DESIGN THINKING			
DESIGN THINKING AS A COGNITIVE STYLE	DESIGN THINKING AS A GENERAL THEORY OF DESIGN	DESIGN THINKING AS DESIGN MANAGEMENT	DESIGN THINKING AS SYNONYMOUS WITH IDEO	DESIGN THINKING AS AN APPROACH TO ORGAN-ISATIONAL PROBLEMS	DESIGN THINKING AS PART OF MANAGEMENT AND INNOVA-TION THEORY
JONES (1972); ALEXANDER (1977); RITTEL (1973); SCHÖN (1983); LAWSON (2005); DORST (2006); CROSS (2006, 2011); AMONG OTHERS.	SIMON (1969); BUCHANAN (1992, 1995); KIMBELL (2011); JOHANSSON-SKÖLBERG ET AL. (2013); ENGHOLM (2020); AMONG OTHERS.	BEST (2006); DE MOZOTA (2006); COOPER & JUNGINGER ET AL. (2011); AMONG OTHERS.	BROWN (2008, 2009, 2015); BROWN & WYATT (2010); BROWN & MARTIN (2015); AMONG OTHERS.	MARTIN (2004, 2009); DUNNE & MARTIN (2006); DUNNE (2015); AMONG OTHERS.	BOLAND & COLLOPY (2004); PLATTNER, MEINEL & LEIFER (2011–2018); LEIFER, PLATTNER & MEINEL (2014); MEINEL & LEIFER (2019); NEY & MEINEL (2019); AMONG OTHERS.

Overview of design thinking and some of the key figures who have contributed to defining the many discourses and approaches.

The model and the chapters in this book offer an overview of current schools of research and practice in design thinking and of the distinctions between them, although the specific breakdown into chapters and columns obviously does not reflect the dynamic character and often fluid transitions of real-life developments. As outlined in the book, the field of design thinking is very broad indeed and will probably never lose its highly heterogenous character. Thus, it is not possible to specify an exclusive or privileged area for research and practice in design thinking. The field is continuously developing, and new disciplines and areas of professional expertise are constantly emerging.

The intention of the book is not to highlight any positions as 'truer' than any others but instead to contribute to a more nuanced debate about the nature and capacity of design thinking, in part by proposing more discussions of the different theoretical-methodological approaches within the field and in part by encouraging more dialogue across the field. To that end, the contributions from designerly thinking have been explored here in some depth in accordance with the book's ambition of adding nuance to the popular discussions of design thinking and promoting a closer dialogue between the research from the design field itself and the new management-oriented understandings. Hopefully, this will also inspire designerly thinking to learn from the management-oriented approaches, with regard to both their societal and organisational impact and their ability to bring insights and methods from design into play in new cross-disciplinary contexts.

> Hopefully, over time, additional general theories about design thinking will emerge that focus both on outcome and on epistemological and methodological reflections. This would enable design thinking, in its many different incarnations, to move forward with greater confidence and reflection. The vague and, as yet, few fully engaged cross-disciplinary discussions do have a potential to develop new experiences in the space in between positions and thus broadly contribute to strengthening design thinking in theory and practice.

From the perspective of this book, however, the key purpose of studies and applications of design thinking should be to enable design thinking to engage more with real-life challenges in a cross-disciplinary effort to develop specific proposals for how these challenges can be investigated and addressed. Going forward, design as thinking and practice should therefore above all remain conscious of its practice dimension by not only presenting its results in written reflections, such as this book, but also in concrete examples. 'Publish or perish' is a common dictum in research. In a design thinking context, the similar imperative would be 'demonstrate or die'!

> To maintain a dual research and practice orientation, naturally, design thinking has to operate in open settings and in projects where the end result is, by necessity, unknown, but where relations and proposals are interactive and emerging. That may seem unrealistic, but upon closer reflection it may be precisely what characterises design thinking: an open-ended exploration of possibilities.

4.1.
Design thinking as activism

The design theorist Ezio Manzini famously said that design can lead to either creation or destruction. Thus, he and several other design theorists argue that the design profession should be charged with coming up with solutions to deal with the climate crisis, which is perhaps the most absolute, almost inconceivable manifestation of a design problem. As a discipline that is engaged in exploring what does not exist yet, design practice should be imbued with a stronger sense of an ethical responsibility: a sense of responsibility that should not merely be manifested in mission statements but also in practical activism.

Some may feel that the expansive concepts of design, with the claim that 'everything is design', have served to undermine the field. Simon's original concept of the artificial world is no longer primarily about the development of artefacts but about design on every scale and including all types of artefacts, plans, constructions, media and interactions. Perhaps, the many and recurring discussions about the nature of design and design thinking could be replaced by an understanding that design thinking does not always take place in a designed, artificial world and thus has been practised from the inside out, as Simon proposed. Instead, it may be a thinking that engages in close dialogue with the nature that design depends on and is itself a reflection of.

As early as during the 1980s, Manzini advocated a more holistic understanding of the man-made world, described with a metaphor of the 'artificial ecology', which moved the focus from the design of artefacts to an interest in the systems, practices and social and cultural settings that the design practice has to engage in with a view to developing more socially and environmentally sustainable cultures of living.

The design theorist Viveka Turnbull Hocking has similarly argued that sustainable design should take place 'beyond the artefact' and instead encapsulate the ways in which design and design thinking can, broadly speaking, help shape new practices for our everyday lives.[87] Hocking proposes a model with three systems that designers and design thinkers need to consider and address in the development of design.

The first of these is 'natural': the interrelated systems of biosphere, hydrosphere, atmosphere and lithosphere.

The second is the 'artificial' system: the integrated landscapes of artefacts as described, for example, as the ecology of the artificial (the man-made) by Manzini (1992) and Krippendorff (2006), among others.

The third is the 'un-natural' system: the interconnected web of understanding of thought, theories and concepts, as described, for example, by Gregory Bateson's 'ecology of mind' (1972), Willard Van Orman Quine's 'web of belief' (1951) and Gilles Deleuze and Félix Guattari's 'rhizomatic network' (1987).

Arguably, many of the problems we are currently facing stem from our tendency to relate solely to our own artificial world — our own artificial world — in materialised as well as immaterial conceptualised manifestations — has been regarded as a resource we can simply consume with no thought of giving anything, besides waste.

Aicher writes in his 1991 book *Die Welt Als Entwurf* (published in English as *The World as Design* in 1994) that 'we are becoming aware that man, whether for good or bad, has stepped outside nature. He is bound to it, but he builds a second world over it, that of constructions'. Aicher argues that in our exclusive focus on achieving 'self-decision' we have detached ourselves from the important alliance with 'universals' in favour of following 'our own ends'. These goals, Aicher writes, have 'turned out to be as dare-devil as they are fatal and we would have to accept it if, because of our constructive autonomy, mankind were to cease to exist in the next century'.[88]

It is thus imperative that we alter our thinking fundamentally and cooperate on creating new sustainable approaches to design development.

Homocentric design. 'Design, stripped to its essence, can be defined as the human capacity to shape and make our environment in ways without precedent in nature, to serve our needs and give meaning to our lives,' wrote the design theorist John Heskett in 2002. Today, we need thinking about design that is not only about fulfilling mankind's needs but also about developing new, sustainable cultures of living. That requires us to abandon the Anthropocene homocentrism that has characterised developments in society and production since the advent of industrialism in the mid 18th century and move towards a paradigm based or more holistic design thinking. The result of humanity's presence on the planet already resembles the destruction left behind by an invasive species that may, in our case, soon have made itself extinct because it was too stupid and greedy to understand the ecosystem it was a part of and depended on.

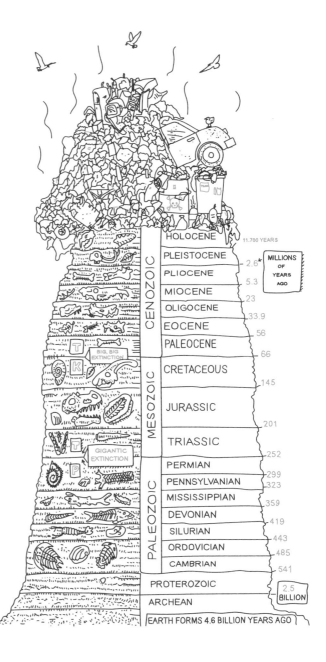

HOLOCENE — 11.700 YEARS

MILLIONS OF YEARS AGO

CENOZOIC
PLEISTOCENE — 2.6
PLIOCENE — 5.3
MIOCENE — 23
OLIGOCENE — 33.9
EOCENE — 56
PALEOCENE — 66

MESOZOIC
CRETACEOUS — 145
JURASSIC — 201
TRIASSIC — 252

PALEOZOIC
PERMIAN — 299
PENNSYLVANIAN — 323
MISSISSIPPIAN — 359
DEVONIAN — 419
SILURIAN — 443
ORDOVICIAN — 485
CAMBRIAN — 541

PROTEROZOIC — 2.5 BILLION
ARCHEAN

BIG, BIG EXTINCTION

GIGANTIC EXTINCTION

EARTH FORMS 4.6 BILLION YEARS AGO

4.2.
From human-centred to life-centred design thinking

Design practices can transform the world, also in physical ways, and thus shape people's behaviour and living conditions. That gives practitioners of design and design thinking a special responsibility, not only in relation to humanity but in relation the planet as a whole. Thus, future design thinking should not only be assessed on how *human*-centred it is, or how well suited it is to meet our fundamental *human* needs in a meaningful manner; it should also be assessed on how much it contributes to the preservation of the biodiversity and the climate conditions without which we cannot design anything at all.

Rather than speaking of *human-centred* design we should perhaps speak of *life-centred* design: design that is sustainable, in every regard, in relation to the natural conditions design is based on and reflects.

For designers, this invites a rediscovery of matter itself: materiality, the stuff of the planet.

In contemporary philosophy, we are seeing the emergence of new approaches, such as new materialism and actor-network theory, which view objects, materials, human beings, systems and nature as equal and interrelated in networks of presencing and emerging. Whether they are viewed as a new form of metaphysics, animism or speculative realism, the new approaches invite a discussion of the relations between the human and non-human domains and between humanity and nature.

The design theorist Tony Fry (2010) argues that the problems we currently face cannot be solved within the epistemological and cultural frameworks that created them. That would only lead to pseudo-solutions. Thus, we need new epistemological approaches capable of challenging our usual ideas about what is material or, perhaps rather, what sort of matter has value in design.

4.3.
Design as avant-garde discipline

Walter Gropius, the director of Bauhaus, called design an avant-garde discipline, and the goal of the Bauhaus School was to set new agendas for the design in the industrialised world that was taking shape at the time.

Indeed, history is full of examples of designers who have played a central role in society as pioneers who formulated comprehensive new visions for the world: from the grandiose visions of heroic functionalism to the self-reflections of the post-war era, which set out to examine the approaches, abilities and capacities that might shape innovative new conceptualisations — what the philosopher Nelson Goodman called *Ways of Worldmaking* (1978).

Today there appears to be a need for a new social indignation like the one motivating the Bauhaus School and the heroic avant-garde movements, which developed the prototypes for the world we live in today — for better or worse. In that regard, it is worth reminding ourselves that design and design thinking are not activities that take place in product development alone; through a profound engagement with systemic, strategic and societal decision-making they can also have a 'worldmaking' character. Moreover, it is important to remember that design and design thinking, in all their forms, are not the exclusive domain of designers but activities that can be practised in many different ways and with very different objectives and mediations.

In his book *Design, When Everybody Designs* (2015), Manzini distinguishes between 'expert design' (carried out by trained designers) and 'diffuse design' (carried out by anyone) and describes how the two modes can interact. The expert designer's role is to take on a central role in society and help facilitate meaningful social and sustainable change. Diffuse design describes the capacity for design that anyone, in principle, possesses, and which expert designers can engage as social actors in a variety of development tasks, with society as one big laboratory for social and environmental innovation.

These collaborative efforts require designers to be able to handle many different scales, formats and timeframes in a transformative process where some aspects are preserved, while others are modified or removed.

Society as design laboratory. In today's rapidly changing world, trained designers, according to Manzini, have a role to play in facilitating processes that can help bring about social and environmental change. This may happen via co-design processes where 'expert designers' facilitate individual or collective groups, communities or organisations in prototyping activities that generate capacity for change. The result of these joint experiments is 'diffuse design', and if successful they can help generate socially and environmentally sustainable initiatives.

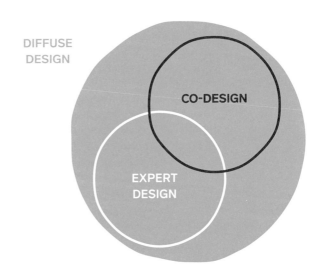

Design as integrative discipline. In 1992, Buchanan described design as a discipline that integrates many different disciplines by connecting fields from the technical sciences, the humanities and the arts, often in unorthodox ways. Buchanan thus suggests that we design a new meta-liberal art, capable of integrating and coordinating other knowledge forms and arts, thus, in principle, taking on a superior role. In line with Buchanan's thinking it is obvious to see design thinking as an integrative, coordinating discipline, an idea that echoes the visions of older design avant-gardists such as Gropius and Maldonado. In a contemporary context, this idea is supported by new co-creative approaches that can facilitate the development of shared visions of what the world could or should look like.

In his book *Designing Regenerative Cultures* (2016) Daniel Christian Wahl introduces the notion of 'Three Horizons' thinking as a framework for organisational and societal development. Wahl describes the dual task of keeping our organisations operational while we transform them to become more sustainable: we need to keep the lights on and maintain focus on day-to-day tasks while also keeping the long-term horizon of visionary and development activities.

Translated into management types, Horizon 1 thinking, according to Wahl, is synonymous with 'business as usual', preserving and maintaining the status quo. Horizon 2 thinking is entrepreneurial and involves seeing potentials within the scope of what is considered possible. Horizon 3 thinking is about visionary leadership and the courage to spearhead fundamental transformation.

According to Wahl, design thinking has potentials on all three levels, but it promises to be the discipline that can help us engage in long-term planning in a short-sighted world. It involves a trial-and-error approach to life and work, which necessarily has to make room for mistakes and wrong turns, but where we never lose sight of the long-term goal.

That takes experimentation, knowledge sharing and collaborative efforts across professions, disciplines and organisations, where design thinking is allowed to be the discipline that coordinates areas of expertise and acts as the creative, generative bridge between the present and the preferred future.

Applied complexity. In a contemporary understanding of design it has to be clear that design as thinking and practice across approaches must be about applied complexity. And, not least, about daring to seek new paths, not only by discovering them but also by creating them. In that regard, design thinkers have the potential to become the visionaries who can ensure the continuation of our world in a way that is compatible with the survival of our biosphere.

Appendix

References

Aicher, O. (1991). *Die Welt als Entwurf*. John Wiley & Sons.

Alexander, C., Ishikawa, S. & Silverstein, M. (1977). *A Pattern Language: Towns, Buildings, Construction*. Oxford University Press.

Argawal, A. & Salunkhe, U. (2012). Impact of Including Design Thinking Competencies in Management Education – An experimental study. In *Leading Innovation Through Design. International Design Management Research Conference*. August 8-9 2012. Boston, USA (pp. 981–988).

Badke-Schaub, P. G., Roozenburg, N. F. M. & Cardose, C. (2010). Design Thinking: A Paradigm on Its Way From Dilution to Meaninglessness?. In K. Dorst et. al (eds.). *Proocedings of the 8th Design Thinking Research Symposium* (DTRS8), pp. 39–49.

Bason, Christian (2017). *Leading Public Design. How Managers Engage with Design to Transform Public Governance*. PhD Dissertation. Copenhagen Business School.

Bateson, G. (1972). *Steps to an Ecology of Mind*. University of Chicago Press.

Beckman, Sara L., & Barry, Michael (2007). Innovation as a learning process: Embedding design thinking. *California Management Review*, 50(1), pp. 25–56.

Best, Kathryn (2006). *Design Management. Managing Design Strategy, Process and Implementation*. Ava Books.

Boland, Richard & Collopy, Fred (2004) *Managing as Designing*. Stanford University Press.

Brandt, Eva & Binder, Thomas (2016). Med det Sociale som Designmateriale. In Lars Dybdahl (ed). *Dansk design nu*. Strandberg Publishing, pp. 354–361.

Brown, Tim (2008). Design Thinking. *Harvard Business Review*, June Issue 2008, pp. 85–93. Retrieved from https://hbr.org/2008/06/design-thinking (last accessed April 2020).

Brown, Tim (2009). *Change by Design: How Design Thinking Transforms Organizations and Inspires innovation*. Collins Business.

Brown, Tim (2015). When Everyone Is Doing Design Thinking, Is It Still a Competitive Advantage? *Harvard Business Review*, 27 August 2015. Retrieved from https://hbr.org/2015/08/when-everyone-is-doing-design-thinking-is-it- still-a-competitive-advantage. (last accessed April 2020).

Brown, Tim & Wyatt, Jocelyn. (2010). Design Thinking for Social Innovation. *Development Outreach, 12* (1), pp. 29–43.

Brown, Tim & Martin, Roger (2015). Design for action. *Harvard Business Review, 93*(9): 57–64. Retrieved from https://new-ideo-com.s3.amazonaws.com/assets/files/pdfs/news/DesignForAction.pdf (last accessed April 2020).

Buchanan, Richard (1992). Wicked Problems in Design Thinking. *Design Issues, 8* (2), pp. 5–21.

Buchanan, Richard (1995). Rhetoric, Humanism, and Design. In Richard Buchanan & Victor Margolin (eds.). *Discovering Design: Explorations in design studies*. University of Chicago Press, pp. 23–66.

Buchanan, Richard & Margolin, Victor (eds.), (1995). *Discovering Design: Explorations in design studies*. University of Chicago Press.

Buchanan, Richard (2001). Design Research and the New Learning. *Design Issues, 17* (4), pp. 3–23.

Budds, Diana (2017). Want to Be A Great Designer? Ban Post-It Notes. *Fast Company*. 25 October 2017. https://www.fastcompany.com/90147380/want-to-be-a-great-designer-ban-post-it-notes (last accessed April 2020).

Bürdeck, Bernhard, E. (1991). *Design – Geschichte, Theorie und Praxis der Produktgestaltung*. DuMont Verlag.

Buxton, Bill (2007). *Sketching User Experience – Getting the Design Right and the Right Design*. Elsevier.

Bødker, Mads (2018). Dystre Tanker om Design Thinking. *Kforum*, 25 October 2018. https://www.kommunikationsforum.dk/artikler/Common-sense-sat-paa-formel (last accessed April 2020).

Carlgren, L., Rauth, I., & Elmquist, M. (2016). Framing Design Thinking: The Concept in Idea and Enactment. *Creativity and Innovation Management, 25* (1), pp. 38–57.

Cooper, Rachel & Junginger, Sabine (2011). *The Handbook of Design Management*. Bloomsbury.

Cross, Nigel (1984). *Developments in Design Methodology*. Wiley-Blackwell.

Cross, Nigel (2006). *Designerly Ways of Knowing*. Springer.

Cross, Nigel (2011). *Design Thinking: Understanding How Designers Think and Work*. Berg Publishers.

de Mozota, Borja (2003). *Design Management. Using Design Build Brand Value and Corporate Innovation*. Allworth Press.

Deleuze, Gilles & Guattari, Félix (French 1980, published in English 1987). *A Thousand Plateaus: Capitalism and Schizophrenia*. University of Minnesota.

Dorst, Kees (2006). Design Problems and Design Paradoxes. *Design Issues, 22* (3), pp. 4–17.

Dorst, Kees (2011). The Core of 'Design Thinking' and Its Application. *Design Studies, 32* (6), pp. 521–532.

Dorst, Kees (2015). *Frame innovation: Create new thinking by design*. MIT Press.

Dunne, David (2018). *Design Thinking at Work: How Innovative Organizations Are Embracing Design*. University of Toronto Press.

Dunne, David & Martin, Roger (2006). Design Thinking and How It Will Change Management Education: An Interview and Discussion. *Academy of Management Learning & Education, 5* (4), pp. 512–523.

Engholm, Ida (2011). Positions in Contemporary Design Research. *Design Research Journal, 2* (11), pp. 48–63.

Engholm, Ida (2017). Reflecting Contemporary Design Research. *Form Akademisk, 10* (3), pp. 1–15.

Engholm, Ida (2018). Designtænkning: et Banalt Innovationsteater? *KForum*, 29 November. https://www.kommunikationsforum.dk/artikler/ Nuancering-af-designtaenkningsbegrebet (last accessed April 2020).

Engholm, Ida & Michelsen, Anders (2016). Er Alt Design? Design Som Tænkning. In Lars Dybdahl (ed). *Dansk design nu*. Strandberg Publishing.

Engholm, Ida & Salamon, Karen Lisa (2017). Design Thinking Between Rationalism and Romanticism – a Historical Overview of Competing Visions. *Artifact, IV* (1), pp. 8.E1–8.E18.

Folkmann, Mads N. (2016). *Designkultur. Teoretiske perspektiver på design*. Samfundslitteratur.

Fry, Tony (2010). *Design as Politics*. Bloomsbury.

Fuller, R. Buckminster (1961). The Architect as World Planner. *Congress of the International Union of Architects*, London. https://arch629eldridge.files.wordpress.com/2010/04/ wk13-bucky-architect-as-world-planner.pdf (last accessed April 2020).

Goldschmidt, Gabriela (2015). Ubiquitous Serendipity: Potential Visual Stimuli are Everywhere. Published at *Research Gate*. January. https://www.researchgate.net/publication/266181774_ Ubiquitous_Serendipity_Potential_Visual_Design_ Stimuli_are_Everywhere (last accessed April 2020).

Halse, J., Brandt, E., Clark, B., & Binder, T. (2010). *Rehearsing the Future*. The Danish Design School Press.

Hassi, Lotta & Laakso, Miko (2011). Conceptions of Design Thinking in the Design and Management Discourses. In *Prodeedings of IASDR, the 4th World Conference on Design Research*. 31 October–4 November 2011. Delft, the Netherlands.

Heskett, John (2002). *Toothpicks and Logos. Design in Everyday Life*. Oxford University Press.

Heskett, John (2005). *Design – A very short Introduction*. Oxford University Press.

Hocking, Viveka Turnbull (2009). An Ecology for Design. From the Natural, Through the Artificial, To the Un-Natural. *Design Principles and Practices. An International Journal, 3* (1), pp. 41–45.

Ignatius, Adi (ed.). (2015). The Evolution of Design Thinking. *Harvard Business Review*, September Issue, pp. 55–85.

Jensen, Hans-Christian (2005). *Fra Velfærd til Designkultur. Velfærdsengagementet i Dansk Designteori og Designpraksis i det 20. Århundrede*. PhD dissertation. University of Southern Denmark.

Johansson-Sköldberg, Ulla, Woodilla, Jill & Çetinkaya, Mehves (2013). Design Thinking: Past, Present and Possible Futures. *Creativity and Innovation Management*, 2 (2), pp. 121–146.

Jones, John Christopher (1970). *Design Methods – Seeds of Human Futures*. John Wiley.

Jones, John Christopher & Thornley, Denis (eds.), (1963). *Conference on Design Methods*. Oxford University Press.

Junginger, Sabine & Faust, Jürgen (2016). Designing Business and Management. Bloomsbury.

Kilian, Jennifer, Sarrazin, Hugo & Yeon, Hyo (2015). Building a Design-Driven Culture. *McKinsey Digital*. https://www.mckinsey.com/business-functions/marketing-and-sales/our-insights/building-a-design-driven-culture (last accessed April 2020).

Kimbell, Lucy (2011a). Rethinking Design Thinking: Part 1. *Design and Culture*, 3 (3), pp. 285–306.

Kimbell, Lucy (2011b). Designing for Service as One Way of Designing Service. *International Journal of Design*, 5 (2), pp. 41–52.

Koskinen, Ilpo, Zimmerman, John, Binder, Thomas, Redstrom, Johan, & Wensveen, Stephan (2011). *Design Research Through Practice: From the Lab, Field, and Showroom*. Elsevier.

Krippendorff, Klaus (2006). *The Semantic Turn: A New Foundation for Design*. Taylor & Francis Group, LLC.

Laursen, Linda N. & Haase, Louise M. (2019). The Shortcomings of Design Thinking When Compared to Designerly Thinking. *The Design Journal*. DOI: 10.1080/14606925.2019.1652531

Lawson, Bryan (2005). *How Designers Think*. Routledge.

Liedtka, Jeanne & Ogilvie, Tim (2012). Helping Business Managers Discover Their Appetite for Design Thinking. *Design Management Review*, 23 (1), pp. 7–13.

Leifer, Larry, Plattner, Hasso & Meinel, Christoph (eds.), (2014). *Design Thinking Research: Building Innovation Eco-Systems*. Springer Science & Business Media.

Lundquist, Jerker (1992). Om Designteorins Uppkomst. *Nordisk Arkitekturforskning*, 4, pp. 7–15.

Maldonado, Tomás (1958). Neue Entwicklungen in der Industrie und die Ausbildung des Produktgestalters, *Ulm*, 2, p. 35.

Manzini, Ezio (1992). Prometheus of the Everyday: The Ecology of the Artificial and the Designer's Responsibility. *Design Issues*, 9 (1), pp. 5–20.

Manzini, Ezio (2008). *Changing the Change; Design, Visions, Proposals and Tools: Proceedings*. Cipolla Carla & Pier Paolo Peruccio (Eds). Allemandi.

Margolin, Victor & Buchanan, Richard (1995). *The Idea of design*. MIT Press.

Martin, Roger (2007). Design and Business, Why Can't We Be Friends? *Journal of Business Strategy*, 28, pp. 6–12.

Martin, Roger (2009). *The Design of Business. Why Design Thinking is the Next Competitive Advantage*. Harvard Business School Press.

Meinel, Christoph, & Leifer, Larry (eds.), (2019). *Design Thinking Research: Looking Further: Design Thinking Beyond Solution-Fixation*. Springer.

Micheli, P., Wilner, S. J., Bhatti, S. H., Mura, M. & Beverland, M. B. (2019). Doing Design Thinking: Conceptual Review, Synthesis, and Research Agenda. *Journal of Product Innovation Management*, 36 (2), pp. 124–148.

Michlewski, Kamil (2016). *Design Attitude*. Routledge.

Ney, Steven & Meinel, Christoph (2019). *Putting Design Thinking to Work: How Large Organizations Can Embrace Messy Institutions to Tackle Wicked Problems*. Springer.

Nussbaum, Bruce (2013). *Creative Intelligence: Harnessing the Power to Create, Connect, and Inspire*. Harper Collins.

Nussbaum, Bruce (2011). Design Thinking is a Failed Experiment. So What's Next. *Fast Company*. 4 May 2011. http://www.fastcodesign.com/1663558/design-thinking-isa-failed-experiment-so-whats-next (last accessed April 2020).

Norman, Don (2013). Rethinking Design Thinking. *Core77. com*. 19 March 2013. https://www.core77.com/posts/24579/rethinking-design-thinking-24579 (last accessed December 2019).

Orr, David (2016). Foreword. In Wahl, Daniel Christian. *Designing Regenerative Cultures*. Triarchy Press, p. 11ff.

Papanek, Victor (1984). *Design for the Real World*. Academy Chicago Publishers.

Papanek, Victor (1970). Om Design og om Undervisning i Design. *Mobilia*, 182, pp. 3–14.

Plattner, Hasso, Meinel, Christoph, & Leifer, Larry (eds.). (2011). *Design Thinking: Understand – Improve – Apply*. Springer Science & Business Media.

Plattner, Hasso, Meinel, Christoph, & Leifer, Larry (eds.). (2012a). *Design Thinking Research: Studying Co-Creation in Practice*. Springer.

Plattner, Hasso, Meinel, Christoph, & Leifer, Larry (eds.). (2012b). *Design Thinking Research: Measuring Performance in Context*. Springer.

Plattner, Hasso, Meinel, Christoph, & Leifer, Larry (eds.). (2015). *Design Thinking Research: Building Innovators*. Springer.

Plattner, Hasso, Meinel, Christoph, & Leifer, Larry (eds.). (2016a). *Design Thinking Research: Making Design Thinking Foundational*. Springer.

Plattner, Hasso, Meinel, Christoph, & Leifer, Larry (eds.). (2016b). *Design Thinking Research: Taking Breakthrough Innovation Home*. Springer.

Plattner, Hasso, Meinel, Christoph, & Leifer, Larry (eds.). (2018). *Design Thinking Research: Making Distinctions: Collaboration versus Cooperation*. Springer.

Quine, W. V. & Ullian, J. S. (1951/1978). *The Web of Belief*. McGraw-Hill Education.

Rasmussen, Jørgen, Kramp, Gunnar & Schiønning Mortensen, Bo (2012). Prototyping Design and Business. *DPPI '11*. Milano IT. 22–25 June 2012.

Rittel, Horst W. J. (1972). *The DMG 5th Anniversary Report*. DMG Occasional Paper, No. 1, January 1972. (Also published in *Design Issues, 23* (1).)

Rittel, Horst W. J. & Webber, Melvin M. (1973). Dilemmas in General Theory of Planning. *Policy Sciences*, 4, pp. 155–169.

Rittel, Horst W. J. (1972). On the Planning Crisis: Systems Analysis of the 'First and Second Generations'. *Bedrifts Økonomen*, 8 (October 1972).

Rossi, Sergio Pavanello (2019). Brainstorming, Post-its and the Killing of New Ideas. *Medium: The startup*. 21 January 2019. https://medium.com/swlh/brainstorming-post-its-and-the-killing-of-new-ideas-1d5d19b1dc95 (last accessed April 2020).

Sanders, Elisabeth B.-N. & Stappers, Pieter Jan (2012). Co-Creation and the New Landscape of Design. *CoDesign*, 4 (1), pp. 5–18.

Sennet, Richard (2009). *The Craftsman*. Penguin Books.

Sheppard, Benedict, Kouyoumjian, Garen, Sarrazin, Hugo & Dore, Fabricio (2018). The Business Value of Design. *McKinsey Quarterly*, (October 2018).

Simon, Herbert (1969). *The Sciences of the Artificial*. The MIT Press.

Schön, Donald (1983). *The Reflective Practitioner: How Professionals Think in Action*. Temple Smith.

Tischler, Linda (2009). IDEO's David Kelley on 'Design Thinking'. *Fast Company*. 2 October 2009. https://www.fastcompany.com/1139331/ideos-david-kelley-design-thinking (last accessed April 2020).

Verganti, Roberto (2009). *Design-Driven Innovation: Changing the Rules of Competition by Radically Innovating What Things Mean*. Harvard Business School Publication.

Volf, Mette (2009). *Design – Proces og Metode*. Systime.

Wahl, Daniel Christian (2016). *Designing Regenerative Cultures*. Triarchy Press 2016.

Wylant, Barry (2010). Design Thinking and the Question of Modernity. *The Design Journal*, 13, pp. 217–231.

Endnotes

1   *Harvard Business Review* (September
    2015). Further, see, e.g., McKinsey
    Digital: *Building a Design-Driven
    Culture* (September 2015); *McKinsey
    Quarterly* (October 2018).
2   See, e.g., Kimbell (2011a).
3   Papanek (1970).
4   See, e.g., Kimbell (2011b).
5   Kimbell (2011a: 285–306).
6   Johansson-Sköldberg, Woodilla &
    Çetinkaya, hereafter Johansson-
    Sköldberg et al. (2013: 121).
7   Jensen (2005: 100).
8   In addition to Kimbell & Johansson-
    Sköldberg et al., see, e.g., Laursen &
    Haase (2019).
9   Johansson-Sköldberg et al. (2013: 121).
10 Ibid.: Regarding the concepts of 'the
    traditional design thinking approach'
    and 'the new design thinking
    movement', see, e.g., Badke-Schaub,
    Roozenburg & Cardoso (2010) and
    Hassi & Laakso (2011).
11 See, e.g., Johansson-Sköldberg et al.
    (2013); Carlgren, Rauth & Elmquist,
    hereafter Carlgren et al. (2016).
12 Nygaard Folkmann (2016: 19).
13 Ibid.: 20.
14 Ibid.: 20.
15 Ibid.: 20.
16 Simon (1969: 111).
17 Alexander (1964: 15).
18 Lawson (2005: 112).
19 Johansson-Sköldberg et al. (2013: 123).
20 Fuller (1961).
21 Simon (1969: 111).
22 Johansson-Sköldberg et al. (2013: 123).
23 Ibid.: 124.
24 Ibid.
25 See, e.g., Jones & Thornley (1963);
    Kimbell (2011a).
26 Maldonado (1958: 35).
27 See, e.g., Cross (1984); Lundquist
    (1992); Lawson (2005); Engholm
    (2011, 2017). For a description of the
    origins and early history of design
    method studies and the so-called
    Design Methods movement, see also
    Jones & Thornley (1963) and Design
    Research Society/History of DRS:
    *http://www.designresearchsociety.
    org/joomla/index.php/about/history.
    html* (last accessed May 2019).
28 Ibid.

29 Rittel & Webber (1973).
30 Bürdeck (1991).
31 Buchanan (1992: 8–14).
32 Ibid.: 16.
33 Buchanan (2001: 9ff).
33 Cross (2011: 147).
35 Norman (2013: unpaginated).
36 British Design Council, Double
    Diamond Model, *https://www.
    linkedin.com/pulse/design-thinking-
    double-diamond-patrick-leinen/* (last
    accessed August 2019).
37 Buxton (2007).
38 Lawson (2005: 289–301).
39 Cross (2011: 78).
40 See, e.g., Engholm (2017).
41 The Utzon example inspired by Volf
    (2009).
42 Dorst (2011: 525–526).
43 Dorst (2015: 49).
44 Cross (2006: 12ff).
45 Ibid.: 92.
46 Sanders & Stappers (2008).
47 Halse et al. (2010).
48 Ibid.: 178.
49 VanPatter & Pastor (2019).
50 The criticism of Post-it notes has
    mainly been expressed in popular
    publications and blogs, which have
    focused on the way in which the
    method separates thinking from
    design (e.g., Budds (2017); Rossi
    (2019).
51 Sanders & Stappers (2008: 7).
52 Koskinen et al. (2011).
53 Ibid.: 5.
54 Brandt & Binder (2016).
55 Engholm & Salamon (2017).
56 Goldschmidt (2015: 8).
57 Ibid.
58 Kant quoted from Sennett (2009:
    149ff).
59 Sennett (2008: 172).
60 Krippendorff (1989: 15, 37).
61 Ibid.: 14.
62 Verganti (2009).
63 Johansson-Sköldberg et al. (2013: 123).
64 See, e.g., de Mozota (2003); Best
    (2006); Cooper & Junginger et al.
    (2011); Bason (2017).
65 Bason (2012: 263ff).
66 The model is inspirered by Best (2006).
67 David Kelley in Tischler (2009).
68 Brown (2008: 87).

69   As cited in Carlgren et al. (2016: 40).
     See also Micheli, Wilner, Bhatti,
     Mura & Beverland (2018: 5).
70   Brown (2008: 88–89).
71   Ibid.: 86.
72   Johansson-Sköldberg et al.
     (2013: 127); Hassi & Laakso (2011).
73   Martin (2009: 5).
74   Dunne & Martin (2006: 513).
75   Martin (2009: 62).
76   Ibid.: 30.
77   Ibid.: 133.
78   See, e.g., Beckman & Barry (2007);
     Argawal & Salunkhe (2012).
79   See, e.g., criticism of the unambiguous
     understanding raised by Carlgren et al.
     (2016: 39).
80   Ibid.
81   Boland & Collopy (2004: 8–9).
82   Ibid.: 17.
83   Johansson-Sköldberg et al. (2013: 129).
     The concept of design attitude has
     been discussed more in depth by Kamil
     Michlewski (2015), among others.
84   Plattner, Meinel & Leifer (eds.)
     (2011: Introduction).
85   Ibid.
86   Criticism of the design management
     field's versions of design thinking, see,
     e.g., ibid.: 131; Bødker (2018); Engholm
     (2018).
87   Hocking (2009).
88   Aicher (1991: 182).

Index

Quick guide to design thinking
©2020 Ida Engholm and Strandberg Publishing

SERIES EDITORS
Ida Engholm and Mads Nygaard Folkmann

PROJECT MANAGER
Mille Bjørnstrup

GRAPHIC DESIGN AND COVER
Troels Faber/NR2154

COVER ILLUSTRATION
Ian Bennett

ILLUSTRATOR
Agnes Engholm, p. 1, 10, 13, 16, 21, 32,
36-37, 39, 42, 46, 48, 51, 52, 54, 59-60, 63,
71, 87, 95, 100
NR2154, p. 18, 30, 34, 35, 40, 49, 50, 68-70,
75-76, 79, 85, 90, 99

TRANSLATOR
Dorte H. Silver

PROOFREADER
Sarah Quigley

THE BOOK WAS SET WITH
Lab Grotesque

PAPER
Munken Pure / Munken Pure Rough

IMAGE PROCESSING
Narayana Press, Gylling

PRINTING, AND BINDING
Jelgavas Tipografija

PHOTO CREDITS
Creative Commons, p. 25
HfG-Archiv, Museum Ulm, p. 29
The Utzon Archives / Utzon Center
& Aalborg University, p. 43
Wiley Ink, Inc. Dist. By Andrews Mcmeel
Syndication, p. 101

Printed in Latvia 2024
1st edition, 4rd printing
ISBN 978-87-92949-05-9

Strandberg Publishing A/S
Gammel Mønt 14
DK-1117 Copenhagen K
www.strandbergpublishing.dk